CHURCHES STARTING CHURCHES

CHURCHES STARTING CHURCHES

A New Church Evangelism
Missional Call to Nazarenes Everywhere

By
Bill M. Sullivan
and
USA/Canada Mission Colleagues

Edited by
Neil B. Wiseman

Nazarene Publishing House
Kansas City, Missouri

10   9   8   7   6   5   4   3   2   1

Contents

▷ ▷ ▷

"The New Testament
indicates that
church planting
was the
primary method
the apostles utilized
to fulfill the
Great Commission."
—Daniel Sanchez

▷ ▷ ▷

The Dream Is Coming True

522 New Churches Already Started

NEIL B. WISEMAN

NAZARENES START NEW CHURCHES. They always have from their earliest beginnings—and they still do. As a result, 12,578 congregations exist around the world today. That means Nazarenes have started an average of more than two churches per week over the last 100 years, not counting churches that have been closed.

Near the dawn of the Church of the Nazarene, when merging Holiness groups joined together in 1908 at Pilot Point, Texas, the new denomination had 10,025 members. Even in those days of small beginnings, they dreamed of a time when their fledgling denomination would have churches around the world. Though they had only 226 congregations at that first Pilot Point gathering, they envisioned a time by faith when their family of congregations would have at least one church in every community.

No Difference Between Home and Global

The first general superintendent, Dr. P. F. Bresee, two years before the merging general assembly at Pilot Point, clarified the church's vision for the future: "Our church is preeminently a missionary church. It knows no difference between home and foreign fields—in these days all fields are near."[1]

When they gathered for worship week by week in local congregations, they expected someone would soon be sent somewhere by the Spirit to start a new congregation. Their God-inspired dreams made them believe that God would help them, and He did in abundant measure.

The establishment of new churches continued as the young denomination grew beyond its infancy. In addition to the passion for new-church evangelism in the local congregations, a new phase in starting churches developed. With a passion for winning more people to Christ, district leaders often joined in the establishment of new churches. So in the '20s and '30s, district superintendents also often served as district evangelists/church starters. As they traveled from town to town in their territory, they held revival meetings and tent campaigns that often resulted in a new church being formed. Some started 5 or 6 churches each year; a few started 10 or more churches per year.

Rejoice with the Pioneers

One superintendent, C. B. Jernigan—who himself organized 130 churches across Oklahoma, Kansas, and Texas—was asked by a pastor from another religious group to be placed in an organized Church of the Nazarene. Jernigan wrote to him: "We are looking for men who will take the bull by the horns, break his neck, skin him and make a tent of his hide, and peddle the meat for a living. I know the pasture that the bull runs in, and if you will come over, I will show him to you. Come on."[2]

Their new-church dream is still unfolding. The amazing result is a small group of 226 churches that started a holy fire that has spread over plains, mountains, valleys, seas, and deserts. Their dreams are being fulfilled today with 12,578 congregations in 138 world areas and 1,390,306 church members. Though the church multiplication from 226 to 12,578 congregations seems unbelievable, it is true.

Rejoice and sing and shout a little as you think of how many churches God has helped Nazarenes start since 1908. It is an inspiring story of grace and achievement.

Every Church Started as a New Church

Now, let's bring our praise closer to home. Every Nazarene church was once a new church. Think of it like this: Anytime anywhere people worship or serve in a Church of the Nazarene, they benefit from the efforts of some church starter and core group who began their church.

Every Church of the Nazarene stands as a memorial to someone's vision, sacrifice, and sweat. Some sold farms. Some quit jobs. Some went out under the sky to preach with no security. Some pastors left well-established pulpits to preach holiness. Many risked reputations. Some were even disowned by their families because they became one of those folks who believed in perfect love.

Someone paid a great price to begin your church. Never forget it. And everyone who has come to faith as a result of that church must feel a debt of gratitude to those selfless folks who started it. They were persons of amazing vision, tenacity, and faith.

After pondering the results of their efforts, does it not seem reasonable that every Nazarene owes a debt of gratitude for the church where they worship and serve? As we praise God for bringing the pioneers' dreams to fruition, could it be that a quiet, inner, sobering challenge starts to grow from six unforgettable words of our Master: "Freely you have received, freely give" (Matt. 10:8)?

Could it be that we have received so much we are being challenged by God to help start a new church in return?

HAVE YOU HEARD ABOUT NEWSTART?

NewStart is the name of a new strategy for starting strong churches among Nazarenes. It is a well-researched plan for starting churches the right way. Like the old way, sacrifice, generosity, and grit are required, but NewStart adds significant strengths to church-start efforts by providing assessment and training for potential pastor leaders, thorough demographics, and local church sponsorship. It helps NewStart core groups start with the right leader, in the right place, at the right time. The NewStart strategy has been in operation since 1996, and several hundred churches have been started using this plan.

Churches starting churches is its key component. NewStart strategy encourages and gives permission to pastors and congregations to begin new churches. It calls sponsoring churches to commit to excellence, to sharing personnel, and to providing mentoring oversight. NewStart requires a new-church pastor to have been approved through the assessment program. It calls for financial responsibility and for an agreement that the new church will not be expected to be supported by the district.

Birthing a church, like human parenting and many phases of global missionary work, requires accepting responsibility that sometimes calls for sacrifice. Southern Baptist church-starting leader Daniel Sanchez explains this reality: "The mother church will have to be willing to sacrifice finances and personnel so the new congregation will have what is needed for it to grow. In some cases, the sponsoring church will have to postpone the acquisition of some things that would be desirable, but not absolutely necessary, in order to help the new congregation."[3]

Sounds a lot like human parenting where the parenting couple commits to the needs of a child as the priority over anything they might want or even need.

SOME ARE STILL NOT SURE WHY
WE START NEW CHURCHES

Starting strong new churches has to do with our involvement in Kingdom commitments to win and develop converts. The heart of the issue is passionately stated by David J. Hesselgrave of Trinity Evangelical Divinity School: "Call it what you will. Call it church planting, church development, church growth, or church-extension evangelism. Or call it mission-evangelism. The task is the same anywhere in the world. Any community of people without an accessible church— whether they reside in North America or South Africa—is a mission field. And it is the responsibility of believers in existing churches to fill those spiritual voids with believing congregations."[4]

New Churches Win and Disciple People

Churches must be started for our Lord and for the people for whom the Son of God gave His life. We start churches for Him—the One who owns the Church. We start churches for the millions who do not know Christ. We want to win them, and we want to help them become authentic disciples of Christ.

Evangelism without a church for discipleship often means that new converts never get through spiritual infancy.

General Superintendent Jim L. Bond explains the challenge of starting strong missional churches: "God raised up Nazarene churches so He could use us to help Him transform lives and show people the way to a holy heart. That cause is for today, not just for 100 years ago. The challenge is as new as the gospel and as up to date as tomorrow. And now God is giving every Nazarene minister and every congregation an opportunity to help make this missional movement in Canada and the United States as effective as it has been overseas."[5]

Kingdom Issue

New-church evangelism is a Kingdom issue—it is for building the kingdom of God rather than a self-hoarding of the church we serve. To build God's kingdom begins and ends with total dependence upon Him. This is, of course, a hallmark of holiness teaching that says when we totally surrender ourselves to God, we are finally in a place where He can use us. Our own efforts can never achieve what the gracious God does to transform us and then send us to impact our world for Christ. God puts a passion in our heart for the lost.

The most obvious reason for starting new churches is taking the gospel to where people live. If there is a cultural group of people in a place who have never heard the gospel, then we can all understand the rationale for sending someone to preach the Good News to them. This is a geographical focus.

Likewise, if there is a town several miles away that does not have a church, we can understand the need to start a new congregation in that community. It just makes sense to place a church close enough to people so they can attend. Yet we have a difficult time understanding why there should be multiple churches in the same community.

Let me explain the rationale. Multiple churches provide many points of entry into the kingdom of God. A growing number of newer churches makes it possible to reach the maximum number of people—such as waiters, salespeople, writers, teachers, laborers, bus drivers, doctors, and trash collectors. And people are what authentic evangelism and starting new churches are all about.

Having a multiplicity of churches provides for various group preferences. This is the cultural task. Immigrants, cultural groups, and other persons having unique interests in common are able to find churches that meet their particular needs.

No single church can reach everyone. No two churches can reach an entire population. Sizable numbers and types of churches are required to evangelize most towns and cities.

A Mission Field on Our Doorstep

NewStart provides a way for congregations to minister to the new mission field God is bringing to our doorstep. General Superintendent Jerry D. Porter challenges us with those new massive opportunities and responsibilities: "Hundreds of thousands of persons from other countries have come to our shores seeking freedom and opportunity. Some are from countries where we have for years sent missionaries. These recent immigrants have joined the complex human mosaic of people who have no contact with the church and little understanding of the gospel. . . . Our task is to work to win lost people who live next door and across town. Our challenge is to have the same depth of commitment and the same sacrifice to reach them we have always had to reach people in faraway places like India and Africa."[6]

Eight Important Reasons for Starting Churches

Briefly let me restate the reasons for starting new churches the right way that have been discussed in many different settings throughout our denomination:

1. Biblical mandate. The "go" of the Great Commission must be followed up with the teaching, baptizing, and making of disciples that can only be done through a church.

2. Population and migration explosion. The arrival of new people near our churches means that nearby evangelism becomes as pressing as global evangelism.

3. *Focus.* New churches tend to focus on winning new people, while existing churches tend to maintain the folks they already serve.

4. *Flexibility.* In a changing environment, new churches in their beginning days adapt quicker to the needs and preferences of a community or cultural group.

5. *Nearness.* The closer churches are to where people live, the more likely they are to have the people attend. Of course, established church members are willing to travel greater distances because they are already connected to the church.

6. *Spiritual impact on sponsoring churches.* Starting new churches often inspires the sponsoring church to examine its reason for being and helps motivate persons who have withdrawn from active participation to assist in filling the void caused by those who joined the new church.

7. *Participation.* Starting a new church calls for a commitment of involvement and giving that may not have been required or even necessary at the mother church. While we do not believe in a works kind of salvation, we know persons tend to thrive spiritually when they are busy doing the work of the Lord.

8. *Unreached people.* In a society as secularized as Canada and the United States are, the need for people to be given opportunity to hear the simple but profound message of the gospel has never been more pressing than now. This requires new churches that are a lot like mission stations in overseas missionary efforts.

NewStart is working. Since it was launched in 1997 following in-depth collaboration with all district superintendents, it has moved from being a new concept to being a mainstream evangelism effort of our church. Since its inception, 661 new churches have been started.

Key NewStart Players—You Are Needed

Because every work of God is centered on the gospel at work in relationships, people are the most important part of NewStart. People are needed to start new churches. People are needed to lead new churches. People are needed to support new churches. And reaching people for Christ is what makes new churches viable and strong and growing.

NewStart is intentionally designed to give control, ownership, and responsibility for starting new churches to the local congregation. It seeks to encourage local churches to effectively give themselves to the central mission of every church—to win and disciple converts. That is the central motivation for NewStart—not a new program, not a new ministry, but a renewal challenge to effective evangelism.

These are the key players:

• **Sponsorship pastors.** For the first time in Nazarene history, pastors and local churches have been empowered to start churches. This means many things, but at its heart it gives every pastor the responsibility of listening carefully to what God wants him or her to do to establish new churches locally among the unreached. Winning people to Christ is exciting, wonderful work, and the rewards last forever.

• **Church boards.** Decision groups are needed to lead in starting new churches. Miracles begin to happen when top lay leaders see that starting churches is as important as every other phase of ministry.

• **NewStart pastors.** Pastors are needed who are committed to Kingdom effectiveness. NewStart pastors are those whom God is sending on a mission to do new-church evangelism. The assessment process is an excellent tool in affirming the call, and the College of New Church Knowledge provides training and networking.

• **Core groups.** Laypersons are needed to be members of the core groups who get involved in the details of starting the new work. In some situations certain laypersons may sense God wanting them to take spiritual responsibility for a people group or a neighborhood. Such persons should allow their zeal for the work to develop in an orderly fashion so the parent church can be involved in facilitating the development of the NewStart church. Some laypersons so sense such a burden for a specific place that they will go start a Bible study, and before long it becomes a church.

• **District superintendent.** In starting new churches, one of the first steps is to keep the district superintendent informed and to ask for his or her help as needed. Work to secure this leader's enthusiastic support. The basic understanding is that the local church will work in concert with the district superintendent in matters of funding, site selection, and the development of strategies for a particular geographic area. In NewStart the local congregation and their pastor take full responsibility for starting the new work, but the district approves their plans and facilities. In NewStart churches the district superintendent becomes adviser, mentor, and partner.

• **Everyone.** As a church moves into new-church evangelism, it will need people to go, people to stay and give, and people who are willing to stay with a NewStart church until the work is well established.

HARVESTTIME HAS ARRIVED

Though I am a child of the city, I am fascinated by the focus harvesttime brings into the lives of farmers and their families, neighbors, and communities. When the crop is ready, everything else takes second or third place. All family members, from the oldest to the youngest, are given tasks, and pity them if they don't do their parts. City cousins are pressed into helping. Big equipment is secured, and additional help is hired.

I even heard of a community that pressed the pastor into checking the weight of the harvest grain as it was brought to the elevator. I'm not sure whether they considered that job to be easy enough for a pastor to accomplish—or maybe they thought they could trust him more than anyone else.

As I think about the harvest, I remember a friend who has for many years been away from the wheat country where he was born. But he goes back every year to drive the combine to help bring the ripe harvest in before the storms come.

All my harvest musings are pretty insignificant compared with the spiritual harvest that awaits the contemporary congregation in new-church evangelism. Let's consider some of the harvest directives and promises from Scripture.

▷ ▷ ▷

"What a huge harvest! . . . How few workers! On your knees and pray for harvest hands!"

▷ ▷ ▷

• Harvest calls the Church to intentionally seek more harvest hands. The bottom line of starting new churches is that more church starters called by the Lord will help multiply the Church. Jesus says, "What a huge harvest! . . . How few workers! On your knees and pray for harvest hands!" (Matt. 9:37-38, TM).

• Harvest is nearby. Notice the incredible message for close-by evangelism in this passage: "Jesus sent his twelve harvest hands out with this charge: *'Don't begin by traveling to some faroff place to convert unbelievers.* And don't try to be dramatic by tackling some public enemy. *Go to the lost, confused people right here in the neighborhood.* Tell them that the kingdom is here. Bring health to the sick. Raise the dead.

Touch the untouchables. Kick out the demons. You have been treated generously, so live generously'" (Matt. 10:5-8, TM, emphases added).

• Harvest is a privileged partnership with Jesus. His disciples must have squared their shoulders and deepened their resolve to do what He wanted done when He told them: "We are intimately linked in this harvest work. Anyone who accepts what you do, accepts me, the One who sent you. Anyone who accepts what I do accepts my Father, who sent me. . . . *This is a large work I've called you into, but don't be overwhelmed by it.* It's best to start small. Give a cool cup of water to someone who is thirsty, for instance. The smallest act of giving or receiving makes you a true apprentice. You won't lose out on a thing" (Matt. 10:40-42, TM, emphasis added).

• Harvest may be bigger than we can imagine. Our Lord said about the seed of the gospel, "Some fell on good earth and came up with a flourish, *producing a harvest exceeding his wildest dreams*" (Mark 4:8, TM, emphasis added).

• Harvest produces a life of purpose and meaning. Paul enjoyed reminding the Corinthian church, *"Now he who supplies seed to the sower and bread for food will also supply and increase your store of seed and will enlarge the harvest of your righteousness.* You will be made rich in every way so that you can be generous on every occasion, and through us your generosity will result in thanksgiving to God. This service that you perform is not only supplying the needs of God's people but is also overflowing in many expressions of thanks to God" (2 Cor. 9:10-12, emphasis added).

• Harvest is ready now. John wrote these incredible words, "He thundered to the Angel who held the sharp sickle, 'Swing your sharp sickle. Harvest earth's vineyard. The grapes are bursting with ripeness'" (Rev. 14:18, TM).

The conclusion—or is it the beginning?—of this new-church evangelism dream that is coming true is this: "I [Paul] planted the seed, Apollos watered it, but God made it grow. So neither he who plants nor he who waters is anything, but only God, who makes things grow. The man who plants and the man who waters have one purpose, and each will be rewarded according to his own labor. For we are God's fellow workers; you are God's field" (1 Cor. 3:6-9).

Let's be used by this mighty cause to start a spiritual revolution in our time and to reenergize our churches with what really counts for eternity. Mere belief will not be enough—passion and action are needed now.

▷ ▷ ▷

"In Scripture, Jesus was the master planner whose strategy was to reach out to everyone and save all who would believe."

—Aubrey Malphurs

▷ ▷ ▷

Missional Foundations for NewStart

Mission Is Part of Nazarene DNA

Tom Nees

ONE OF THE FIRST OBSERVATIONS made about the new "missional" theme is that the word can't be found in the dictionary. But we know what it means. Missional brings missions into the life of the church as we know it. Admittedly, there is no precise definition for missional churches and missional leaders. However, the challenge to become missional has generated creative responses from pastors, laity, and other church leaders.

"Missional" is not in the dictionary, but we know what it means.

Perhaps one of the first questions raised when trying to describe a missional church is, "What do missionaries do?" or more importantly, "If our neighborhood or city is a mission field, what should we be doing differently?"

When we think of a mission field, we usually think of an entire country, such as Swaziland, or a region, such as the Balkans. The mission there is to reach as many people as possible throughout the country or region for Christ and the church. Mission strategy involves more than starting single, autonomous congregations. Mission-field churches are started with the expressed understanding that they are a part of a plan to multiply or reproduce themselves in additional congregations. Missional pastoral and leadership training programs are instituted to equip local or indigenous leaders in the multiplication of churches. As local churches gain in numbers and finances, they are always close to the cutting edge of evangelism and outreach as partners, indeed as sponsors of new churches.

There is a humorous story about a district superintendent in Florida who observed a church van on the interstate identified as belonging to a Haitian church from a town on his district. The problem was that the district superintendent did not know of such a church.

Local congregations in Haiti routinely sponsor and start churches on their own. When a new group is ready for recognition, the district is notified. The Haitian work in the Bahamas started this way. The first Haitian congregations in the United States were started by Haitian Nazarene refugees who assumed that the first thing to do in their new surroundings was to start churches. It did not occur to them that they needed to ask for permission.

The work of our missionaries was not simply to start a new church at a particular location, but to reach the city, if not the nation, with many churches.

In 1992 I had the privilege of being in Red Square in Moscow on the first May Day following the collapse of Communism. It happened to be when the first contingent of Nazarene workers was arriving to open our pioneer missionary work in Russia and countries in the former Soviet Union. It seems now like the distant past. It was really only a few years ago that any notion of taking the message of holiness to these countries was thought impossible.

We have followed with great interest the expansion of the work in Moscow and many other of the 138 world areas where the Church of the Nazarene has extended its missionary effort. There, and everywhere else around the world, the work of missions and missionaries is the same—churches are started where believers can be nurtured and lost people drawn to Christ.

The work of our missionaries in Moscow was not simply to start a church at a particular location, but to reach the city, if not the nation, with many churches.

The work of missions is to reach entire cities and countries by starting as many churches as possible. And yet when it comes to the work of ministry in our own neighborhoods and cities, we are often content to simply build our own local congregation—sometimes without plans to respond to the needs of the whole city and the entire nation.

As difficult as it is to reach and retain people, there is a natural tendency to hold on to members and finances in order to grow a congregation as large as possible. Encouraging members to leave in order to start another congregation may seem to be counterproductive until the mission mandate of the church is fully understood. The missional challenge is much more than starting and sustaining autonomous congregations. Congregations are called upon to enter into partnership with one another to reach as many people as possible for Christ and the church, in as many different places and circumstances as possible.

▷ ▷ ▷

Every church gains when it is part of a plan larger than its own existence.

▷ ▷ ▷

I heard one group describe the presence of the church in their city by saying they have one church with many congregations. The missional challenge changes the way in which we think about new churches. In the past, starting a new church usually meant that an existing congregation had to lose members and money in order for another to gain members and money. With a missional mentality, we no longer think of losing and gaining. Every church gains when it is part of a plan larger than its own existence. A missional congregation is not an end in itself. It is always a means to an end—building the Kingdom through obedience to the Great Commission.

There may be an implied threat to existing, mature congregations in the claim that "starting new churches is the most effective means of evangelism we know of" if that implies that an older congregation cannot be missional simply because it is not a new church. The threat is real if we continue to think in terms of gains and losses, of new versus old.

This new missional mentality brings all churches and pastors together around a common commitment. New churches can only be started as they are nurtured and sponsored by existing congregations. The gains of a new congregation are the gains of the sponsor congregation. No one loses in this equation. With their strength, stability, and experience, mature congregations become incubators for missional outreach. They take as much pride in the growth and success of the new congregations they have sponsored as parents do in their children.

▷ ▷ ▷

Missional churches take as much pride in the growth and success of newly sponsored congregations as parents do in their children.

▷ ▷ ▷

This new missional mentality challenges the myth that a local congregation needs to be a certain size and strength before it can begin thinking of sponsoring a new congregation in a needy area or among another group of people. Missional thinking has little if anything to do with size and statistics. It's all about the Kingdom.

It may be that what attracts people to a congregation is its aggressive mission strategy to reach beyond itself. To join a missional congregation is to be on a mission to reach people for Christ and the Kingdom by looking for opportunities to go beyond the walls and programs of the local church. It is to always plan for multiplication. Churches small and large in cities or small towns can be missional.

In a missional church the question is always, "Who among us is God calling to start a Bible study in their home, begin a prayer meeting in a nearby community, start an ESL [English as a second language] class for a minority group, or organize a compassionate ministry program?" All of these activities and more have been the means by which new congregations have been started.

Two themes are at the heart of Nazarene missions. The first is that of being sent. Most of us understand that missional service requires sending someone someplace to reach lost people with the gospel. Second and complementary to the first is that of crossing language, cultural, and belief borders to communicate the message.

Both of these missional themes contribute to NewStart or new-church evangelism. NewStart recognizes that it takes distinctive leadership gifts and graces to start new churches. The core group of members must affirm the call of the NewStart pastor. They, too, are sent. Theirs is a missionary assignment with a divine calling. They are sent to a particular place to begin a new faith community. This new missional mentality challenges mission-minded congregations to be a sent church as well as a sending church.

Cross-cultural ministry, the other fundamental theme of missions, is particularly important for new-church evangelism in the United States and Canada of the 21st century. The new churches of the future will reflect the rich diversity that increasingly characterizes these two countries. Missional thinking encourages every congregation to look for and seek out people from various cultural and language groups. Missionary work has always included crossing borders and oceans, learning languages, and adapting to cultures in order to spread the gospel. While that continues, the motivation to cross cultural and language barriers takes on new dimensions amid the multicultural conditions of the United States and Canada.

Missiologist Chuck Van Engen recently called for a new strategy to start multiethnic churches in the United States and Canada. His article "Is the Church for Everyone?" in the spring 2000 issue of the *Journal of the American Society for Church Growth* challenges many prevailing ideas about starting culturally exclusive congregations. He contends that churches "should strive to be as multiethnic as their surrounding contexts."[1] Van Engen suggests that churches should have the same diversity as the nearby neighborhood schools and shopping areas.

The Great Commission can now be implemented in any American city. In Matt. 28:19, Jesus directs His followers to "make disciples of all nations." The imperative in the verse is not the word "go" but rather "make disciples." It would be better translated as "In your going . . ." or "As you go . . ." or "Wherever you go . . ." Jesus knew that eventually His followers would disperse throughout the world.

The word "go" has been so overemphasized that we sometimes miss the main point of the Great Commission. Some have been led to think that it is only in going to somewhere else that one can be obedient to the missionary call. Jesus instructed His followers to make disciples among all people regardless of where they might find themselves.

In the first chapter of Acts, Jesus gave His followers the plan for missions. They were to be witnesses everywhere the Diaspora might take them. That meant "in Jerusalem, and in all Judea and Samaria, and to the ends of the earth" (v. 8). It is not that one place had more urgency or need than another. The point is that wherever these first believers might find themselves, they were to be "witnesses" empowered by the Holy Spirit.

But an interesting thing happened on the Day of Pentecost. Rather than going to Judea, Samaria, and the ends of the earth, "God-fearing Jews from every nation under heaven" (2:5) came to them. They were able to evangelize the world that day by speaking the Word to the foreigners in their own city.

Our situation is not unlike that. People from every country, every language, and every race have immigrated to the United States and Canada. According to Census 2000, most major American cities are composed of a "majority of minorities" with no one group in the majority. Minorities make up the majority of the accumulated population of the 100 largest cities in the United States and Canada. Diaspora missions is sharing the gospel and starting churches among those who have come to this country as immigrants, knowing that in the normal course of communication and travel they will send the Word to their homeland.

Cross-cultural missions will likely be quite different in the future. In the past, cross-cultural ministry referred for the most part to missionaries from Western so-called Christian countries who learned other languages and cultures. In multicultural America no one can learn all the languages. And there are people from within many of these immigrant minority cultures who are more effective in missional work than anyone from the outside could ever be.

The cultural barrier to cross in the mission field that describes America is more a belief barrier than a cultural barrier. On the belief side of that barrier are people of faith from many different countries and races speaking a variety of languages. The church itself is multicultural. People from many nations are now to be found in the church. It is not unusual for a single congregation to have members from a dozen or more countries.

While they have many cultural differences, they are of one faith. The missionary challenge is to reach out and to welcome lost people from all the nations. On the belief side of the barrier, Christians now find themselves joining hands with fellow believers from a variety of countries. Cross-cultural ministry means something more than white people going to other countries and cultures. In multicultural America missional believers from all backgrounds, minorities included, will have opportunities to reach beyond their own cultural group to share the gospel.

The case for American missions to the ends of the earth is credible only when made from a church as committed to reaching people and starting churches in our own cities as abroad.

Cross-cultural ministry now means joining with believers from various cultures and including them in our missional plans to reach people and start churches within our neighborhoods and cities. This emphasis on missions nearby will not detract from missions faraway. On the contrary, the case for American missions to the ends of the earth is credible only when made from a church as committed to reaching people and starting churches in our own cities as abroad.

Some years ago my wife and I were dinner guests of the ambassador to the United States from Swaziland. We were invited along with Tom and Faye Riley, missionaries to Swaziland. Tom and Faye were spending several weeks of their furlough as missionaries in residence at Washington, D.C., First Church of the Nazarene. Tom knew the ambassador well. He was director of Nazarene schools in Swaziland when the ambassador was in charge of government schools.

A life-size portrait of King Sobhuza hung in the entry of the embassy. I recognized the king immediately. My generation grew up listening to missionaries from Swaziland. Every missionary had a slide presentation with a picture of the Swazi king. I told the ambassador that I felt right at home.

When the ambassador found out that I was the pastor of the First Church of the Nazarene, he began to ask some questions. He was very thankful for the missionaries that the church had sent to his small country to teach, heal, and preach the gospel. He also knew that there were three times as many people of African descent in and around our nation's capital as in Swaziland. He wanted to know what the church was doing—teaching, healing, and preaching—among this large African-American population.

This occurred at a time when I had a growing interest in cross-cultural ministry. That was before we thought of this country as a mission field. I avoided using the language of missions—that was for somewhere else.

Now all that has changed. We know better. The whole world is a mission field. Lost people are just as lost in the United States and Canada as they are in any other world area. A church in Washington, D.C., is as much a missionary outpost as a church in Swaziland. A pastor in Dodge City, Kansas, is as much a missional leader as a pastor in Guatemala. New York, Chicago, Los Angeles, Montreal, and Houston are just as needy as Cape Town, Bombay, Seoul, and Mexico City.

We are a missional church, driven by the Great Commission. And we know that this missional mandate begins where we live—in Jerusalem. So the idea of the United States and Canada as a mission field is not altogether new.

For instance, over 50 years ago several self-funded and self-appointed missionaries went to the Native Americans in the Southwest—particularly the Navajo Nation.

We now have more than 50 churches among Native people and a Native American mission-training center in Albuquerque, New Mexico, preparing effective Native American leaders. All this began with missionaries within our own borders.

We used to talk about home missions. But until recently we were not convinced that we were doing real missionary work unless we crossed an ocean or a border. That, too, has changed. Not only has missions come home, but also many of the converts of our global mission enterprise have come to this country as missionaries to America.

I was startled when John Ndambuki from Kenya joined our Washington, D.C., Community of Hope Church with a clear call to be a missionary to African people in America. He is now the pastor of a new church he started last year—the College Park, Maryland, African congregation, a congregation of immigrants from Kenya and Tanzania.

We used to think that the only real missionaries were those who went to different cultures and learned other languages. That, too, has changed. We now recognize that some of the most effective missionary work is done by Christian leaders within their own culture.

Thanks to the faithfulness of 84 district superintendents and nearly 5,000 pastors, the church in the mission field of the United States and Canada is growing. During the past year, 31,000 new Nazarenes joined our churches. In fact, the church has been growing at that rate for the past four years. Since the last general assembly, more than 100,000 new Nazarenes have joined the church in the United States and Canada. And last year, 103 new congregations reported statistics for the first time. That is double the number of just a few years ago.

The fastest growing segment of the church is among minorities—particularly the immigrant church. One hundred and one new minority churches have been started in the past four years, nearly half of them Hispanic. There have been years when we have started more Spanish-speaking congregations than all the rest combined.

It was just four years ago that we began to recognize the United States and Canada as a mission field. What was once the Evangelism and Church Growth Division is now the USA/Canada Mission/Evangelism Department.

There is growing excitement about the future of missions in the country that has been the driving force of global missions for the past 100 years.

We must now do on this mission field what is being done on every mission field around the world—start new churches to reach lost people. Starting new churches is still the most effective means of evangelism. While we rejoice in the recent growth of the church in the United States and Canada, we recognize the harvest opportunities around us. We can and will do more.

A few months ago I enjoyed a couple of days on the Northwest District with Bob Shea, district NMI (Nazarene Missions International—formerly NWMS) president. As we drove across eastern Washington State, we talked about the tens of thousands of Hispanics who have recently settled there.

Like many of you, Bob has traveled the world with Work and Witness. He is a rancher who in his retirement years has taken on a new vocation. He is a full-time NMI volunteer.

Bob shared his burden for starting churches among Spanish-speaking churches on his own district. And then we began to think—what if our local missionary societies through their prayer network, through their passion for missions, would become catalysts to start new churches in our own towns and cities?

What if Nazarene Missions International—the organization that has helped build the "bridges of God" to lost people around the world—would encourage our local churches to build bridges to those who have moved here from around the world?

Local NMI societies could help pastors do here what we pray for and give for on every mission field—start new churches. Some of these new churches will be led by lay leaders as well as clergy, and by women as well as men. What about an NMI-sponsored new congregation? Why not?

To reach the missional vision cast by the Board of General Superintendents for the Centennial Celebration in 2008, we need to start 1,000 new churches in the United States and Canada during the next seven years. This is a faith projection beyond anything we have done in the recent past. I believe we can do this. We can start 1,000 churches in the next seven years.

We need prayer, we need divine direction, we need called and trained missional leaders, and we need NMI to be a catalyst for new-church evangelism in Canada and the United States.

In his devotional address to the 2001 General Assembly, former General Superintendent and missiologist Dr. Donald Owens introduced his remarks by recalling a question to the editor of *Holiness Today*. A woman from Idaho wrote and asked where the word "missional" originated. Dr. Owens used that question and its answer to introduce his thoughts on the state of missions today—particularly the emphasis on the missional church in the United States. He reminded the church that "we are repudiating the mystical 'doctrine of salt water,' that is, the idea that traveling to foreign lands is the test and criterion of what is truly missionary." He went on to say, "This 'geographical myth' has been our problem. It has not been God's problem."[2]

In the spirit of the Great Commission and the final words of Jesus in Acts 1, we can identify four characteristics of missional churches and leaders. A missional church

- makes disciples of lost people,

- reaches across cultural barriers,

- commits to compassion evangelism,

- reproduces itself in new churches.

Concepts of a Missional District
The Reasons for Partnerships with Local Churches
BILL M. SULLIVAN

A DISTRICT SUPERINTENDENT has the opportunity to lead a group of local churches in a significant accomplishment of the Great Commission. The main task of the district superintendent is to inspire pastors to lead their churches to an effective expansion of the kingdom of God. The organizational structure in which the district superintendent works places him or her in a position to see that the work of the Kingdom gets accomplished. The district superintendent does not do the work, but it is his or her assignment to encourage pastors in their efforts to get it done.

1. Ministry occurs exclusively at the local church level.

All ministry is local. International Headquarters does not perform ministry. That is the work of the local church. Districts do not perform ministry. But districts provide a support system for local churches. Denominational structure, both general and district, exists for the purpose of supporting local churches in Kingdom work.

2. The district provides a network of relationships and resources.

The district system includes a network of relationships and resources that help sustain the local church and the pastor. One service the district provides for the local church is inspiration when discouragement sets in. Often the inability to make progress causes a congregation to become dispirited. They get their eyes on their problems and can't see the evangelistic potential that is all around them. This is when the district superintendent can be of great help. As the saying goes, "A little encouragement can spark a great accomplishment."

3. The district superintendent is a vision maker.

The district superintendent can help the pastor and the church catch a new vision for God's work. A demographic review of the community surrounding the church may be all that is necessary to open their eyes to new possibilities. A district superintendent might say to one of his or her pastors, "Have you thought about sponsoring a new church in that new community?" In many instances the need for a new church in an adjacent community will ignite spiritual fervor in the congregation. The superintendent's guidance may result in a new church being started that wins scores of new people to Christ. The sponsoring church will experience a wonderful sense of fulfillment in starting a new congregation.

4. District growth is the result of starting new churches.

A district superintendent's long-term effectiveness will be linked directly to the number of new churches that are started on the district. Dallas Mucci has seen the Metro New York District more than double as a result of 60 to 70 new churches he has started! Over a 10-year period new churches will contribute more to the growth of a district than any other accomplishment. Growth in district membership, attendance, and finances will result primarily from starting new churches.

5. Effectiveness comes from working through the local church.

Because ministry occurs only at the local church level, district superintendents will need to work through local churches to accomplish district goals. I remember Raymond McClung, who was district superintendent of the Houston District for many years, saying to me, "As a district superintendent, you are always working by remote control." It is difficult for a district to initiate a new church. If they choose an area close to an existing church, they may meet resistance from that church. If they solicit members to become part of the founding core group, they may be viewed as Robin Hoods who steal members from one church in order to start another one. In addition, the multitude of details in beginning a new church is just too great for the district organization to handle. On the other hand, the local church has the personnel and time to stay close to a new church and its needs.

6. Laity make a wonderful support team for a new local church.

Laity from the local church can provide most of the day-to-day support and encouragement the new congregation will need. When we began the church in Rocky Mount, North Carolina, the lay coordinator, Pete Leslie from the Fayetteville church, took care of all of the details of the project. Such simple matters as baby-sitting for the pastor's children or food preparation for a group function are well within the capability of laypersons in a sponsoring church but are almost impossible for a district organization. A sense of ownership is an added benefit of local church involvement in the development of a new church.

7. Sponsoring-church ownership is the foundation of a successful NewStart.

A missional district superintendent realizes that the multiplication of ministry depends on inspiring others to participate. Whenever I explain the real involvement aspect of NewStart, pastors have been eager to participate. The commitment of others hinges on the sense of fulfillment experienced in the involvement. Fulfillment, of course, is the satisfaction resulting from being responsible for an accomplishment. Fulfillment will be diminished to the extent the reward for accomplishment goes to someone other than the persons involved. This is why it is so important for the district to place the sponsorship of a new church in the hands of the local church.

8. There is a vast difference between helping and sponsoring.

The joy of seeing a new church started makes it difficult for a district superintendent to release control to a local church. Who wants to give up the most exciting part of the job! The superintendent may be willing to permit the local church to participate, but participation and sponsorship are two vastly different relationships. Participation means helping the district accomplish its task. Sponsorship means taking responsibility for the challenges, activities, and rewards of getting a new church going. It is sponsorship that ignites the missional interest of both pastor and congregation.

9. You cannot have your cake and eat it too!

The district benefits from all new churches. Additional churches mean more members, larger attendance, and greater financial resources. The district superintendent can rejoice in all of these increases, plus the satisfaction of having inspired local churches to missional involvement. But the district superintendent cannot have it all.

10. The person in charge is sovereign.

If the district superintendent chooses to subtly hold on to sponsorship, the local church will subtly back out of involvement. The reason for this is both personal and political. Either sponsorship carries with it authority and accountability, or it isn't personally challenging, and no pastor is going to risk incurring the wrath of the district superintendent by meddling in his or her business.

11. Sponsorship and control are joined at the heart.

Ownership of the project determines who is the sponsor. I witnessed this early in my ministry when my district superintendent told a neighboring pastor who was starting a new church that he was doing the district's business. If the local church is allowed to sponsor the new church, then control of the project must be given to the local church. If the district superintendent retains control of the project, then the local church will not feel accountable for the new church. Who is finally in control of the new church will determine who makes the greatest investment and who stands by the project through thick and thin.

12. Do the math.

The major reason the local church is the best sponsor for new churches is that there are 65 churches on a typical district but only one superintendent. Do the math. Many more new churches can be started by local church sponsorship than by district sponsorship, and they can be started at a faster rate. The missional heartbeat of a local church can be nurtured but cannot be replaced by the district.

13. Mission churches make a district missional.

It is through the local church that a missional district can most effectively be developed. As the district superintendent inspires pastors and laity to take both the initiative and the responsibility for starting new churches, a widespread missional force will emerge. This is beginning to happen—661 churches were sponsors last quadrennium and 104 last year. As this spreads, new churches will be formed, new converts will be won to Christ, new leaders will be challenged, and new ministries will be created—not to mention the multiplication of resources that will be available to the district as a result.

14. Win-Win!

Everyone in the entire organization wins really big when the district superintendent fills the role of inspiring pastors and local churches to become missional in both word and deed. It is a true "win-win" situation. The advance of the Kingdom among missional churches is enormous. Challenging churches to missional pursuits is easily the most rewarding leadership role in the ecclesiastical hierarchy.

15. Small churches are beautiful.

Before dealing with the specifics of starting new churches, we need to consider two other options. Many Nazarenes, both lay and clergy, believe something needs to be done with the multitude of small, weak churches, such as merging them together. It is true there are many churches in this category, not only in our denomination but also in all denominations. Their prevalence may indicate a structure or characteristic that is preferred by many people. What I have observed in visiting many small churches could lead to that conclusion.

16. The fellowship in small churches is great.

Because of my interest in small churches, I have visited many small congregations across the years. Being a member of a very large church with great services and programs, I wondered if people in small churches were dispirited and unhappy. Much to the contrary, I have been struck by the apparent joy the people in small congregations have in assembling together. Whether the satisfaction was social or spiritual or both wasn't clear. But it was very obvious they were glad to see each other and happy to be together. Such an appearance was very different from what I had expected. Anyone suggesting the merger of small churches must deal with this reality, but there is an even greater factor to consider.

17. One plus one usually equals one!

Mergers seldom work. Typically, after two years, the merged congregation is no larger than the largest church involved in the merger. In other words, a number of people equal to the number in one of the churches simply disappears. In at least one-third of the mergers the decline is even greater. Only in a limited number of mergers does the combined congregation increase significantly.

18. Hang on to property.

The loss of real property is a factor a district superintendent must take into consideration. When two churches merge, the combined church keeps possession of both properties. If one property is sold, the funds go to the church, not to the district. If, as in most cases, the merger doesn't produce any growth or improvement, the district has simply lost funds that could have been invested in a new church that would probably have produced considerable growth. Disorganization is usually the preferred way to deal with a congregation that is no longer viable.

19. Resurrecting a dead church is a miracle too!

Across the years, various attempts at revitalization of weak churches have been attempted. I recall the words of a 20-year veteran district superintendent who said flatly, "Resurrections don't work!" Since revitalizations have seldom been reported, there are no statistics to evaluate the results of renewal efforts. Anecdotal reports are probably available to support both success and failure.

20. Babies are better.

A district superintendent must be flexible and adapt to a variety of circumstances. Only the leader on site can decide what is best in a specific situation. But as a general rule, a new church will produce more favorable results than church mergers or attempted church resurrections.

21. Strengthen the weak.

This is not to say an effort to strengthen weak churches is inappropriate. Indeed, a significant responsibility of any district superintendent is to provide ongoing help and encouragement for all the churches on the district. Many district superintendents provide "Skill Skools" and training seminars for pastors.

A district superintendent must serve all of the churches and direct a comprehensive program. He or she will always have a mix of both strong and weak churches. But there must be an aggressive new-church program to keep the district focused on mission and to replace the losses that are inevitable over time. How to create and maintain an aggressive new-church program is the subject of another chapter.

Practices of a Missional District
Ways to Multiply NewStarts
BILL M. SULLIVAN

IT IS ONE THING to learn missional concepts; it is quite another to put the concepts into practice. In order to develop a missional district, the concepts and practices must come together in a united, highly energized effort. This chapter will consider the practices that are effective in developing a missional district.

1. Coordinators and consultants are helping.

Some districts have retained consultants or hired full-time coordinators to give special attention to starting new churches. Jim Bearden, district superintendent of South Carolina, was one of the first to employ a full-time district NewStart coordinator. David Wines is the district NewStart coordinator. Consultants are also available. Both have proved effective. The task is so crucial to growth that someone needs to be attending to it on a regular basis.

2. Organizing mission zones is a powerful strategy.

The New England District has an outstanding record of starting new churches. District Superintendent Charles Zink has created nine mission areas. Two mission directors lead each area. Their task is to (1) develop a clear mission vision and goals for new churches and growth, (2) create a strong sense of connectedness and unity for the purpose of mission fulfillment in each area, and (3) enhance the supportive network and fellowship in each area.

3. Small churches are sponsoring new churches.

It appears, at least from the reports, that a church of almost any size can be significantly involved in sponsoring a church. During the 1997—2001 quadrennium, 335 of 661 sponsoring churches were under 100 in attendance. Even a NewStart sponsored a new church last year! The assumption is that only larger, stronger churches have the resources to sponsor a new church. The reason that is an erroneous concept is that it assumes financial strength is the primary ingredient. While it is true that money is needed to begin a new church, it is incorrect that the mission is based on funding. The real truth is that money moves to mission. Whenever someone proposes to engage in a mission, there is usually someone else with money who wants to be a part of the mission. Casting a captivating vision for mission will typically call forth the funding necessary to accomplish the mission.

4. There is a form for determining significant sponsorship.

In the packet of materials for the annual pastor's report to the district assembly, there is a form for determining if a church was significantly involved in new-church sponsorship. By following the step-by-step form, the pastor can determine if the church provided (1) a number of attendees for the core group equal to 10 percent of the sponsoring church's membership, (2) financial support equaling 2 percent of Raised for All Purposes, or (3) gifts-in-kind equaling 3 percent of the previous year's Raised for All Purposes. A church may qualify based on any of the three bases.

5. The sponsorship plan is flexible.

Smaller churches may not be able to give members to the core group, but they may be able to contribute a sufficient amount of money or gifts-in-kind. Last year, a church of only 13 was significantly involved in starting a new church! Though it may seem the opposite of what would be expected, larger churches may not be able to give a sufficient percentage of money but may easily provide the necessary number of people for the core group of the new church. The sponsorship plan is flexible enough that every church can be significantly involved in new-church sponsorship.

6. Provide financial incentives for sponsorship.

Local churches are missional by nature, but it is still advisable to give them financial incentives for sponsoring new churches. The original *NewStart Strategy Document* suggested that districts return to sponsoring churches all or a major portion of their home mission budget. Many districts are following this plan. Some districts have a unified budget, and a certain percentage of the district budget is earmarked for home missions. The proper amount returned to the sponsoring church from a unified budget could be calculated based on that percentage. Other districts have no home mission budget at all. In such cases, the district is urged to help as funds permit.

7. Use the funds from the sale of disorganized churches.

Many districts have funds from the proceeds of the sale of disorganized church properties. Most districts have reserved these funds to be used only for helping establish new churches. They are usually invested in the purchase of property but are sometimes used for start-up grants.

8. Home mission booster clubs raise funds for new churches.

Many districts have "booster club" type organizations to help fund new-church starts. I remember when Dr. Jim Diehl became district superintendent of Nebraska. One of the first things he did was to start such a club, which he called his "Start, Strengthen, and Save" club. Two to four times a year a call is made to members of the district home mission club to contribute the amount of money pledged by the club member. Two hundred club members giving an average of $25 per call produces $5,000. While not enough to start a new church, it is adequate to fund the development of a plan to start a new church.

9. Extended subsidies are not a good idea.

The amount of money needed to start a new church will vary from situation to situation. Substantial support at the beginning of the project is better than smaller amounts spread out over a longer period of time. Across a long, expensive history we have learned how difficult it is to wean a church off financial subsidy. After being out of the superintendency for 21 years, I still have flashbacks from trying to take away a long-term subsidy. Regardless of what people think or claim, extended subsidies tend to be harmful instead of helpful. The sooner a new church can function without financial subsidy, the greater is its viability.

10. No subsidy is one of the secrets of small-church sponsorship.

This financial reality partly explains why small churches are successful in sponsoring new churches. They find ways of getting the new church going and gathering financial support from within its own ministry context.

11. Group sponsorship works well.

In many instances, two or more churches will cooperate to sponsor a new church. There may be occasions when an entire zone will work together to begin a new church. In multiple sponsorship, a steering committee of representatives from each church may be helpful.

Usually, however, the chairperson is relied upon to do most of the detail work.

12. Some churches are sponsored across district boundaries.

Special challenges are faced when a church wants to sponsor a new church on another district. This usually occurs in an area where the sponsoring church is located near the district boundary. There are many places where district boundaries cut through major metropolitan areas. Oklahoma City is divided among four districts! This can easily mean a nearby community that needs a new church is on a different district from the sponsoring church. In such circumstances, there should be negotiations between the two district superintendents. The district on which the new church will be located would probably make every effort to invest heavily in the new work, since the sponsoring church will be contributing resources that would normally accrue to the district of which they are a part. It should be noted, however, that in Christian generosity, there may be many instances in which one district contributes significantly to another district without any expectation of return. Such is the nature of love.

13. Many churches can start a new multicultural church.

There is a continually increasing opportunity in America to do evangelism among minority groups. Beginning a church among them can be as simple as forming a Sunday School class or conducting a Bible study. Every Nazarene church in many locations across America could host a minority group church in their facilities. Woodie Stevens, district superintendent of New Mexico, says every church on his district could host a multicultural congregation. Multiple congregations in a single building are an increasing occurrence. This presents special challenges for the host church. New insights are being discovered as increasing numbers of churches become involved. There is much that remains to be learned.

14. Mission offers the new and the daring.

It is easy to build excitement for mission. The very nature of mission generates anticipation. People generally are interested in anything new and intrigued by daring adventures. Mission usually offers both the new and the daring. Beginning a new church is definitely a new adventure.

15. Mission is a magic word.

Mission is also a magic word in Nazarene culture. While some are disenchanted with mission education and organization, few, if any, are disinterested in mission itself. This is amply demonstrated by the success of the Work and Witness program and by continued giving to the World Evangelism Fund. So the district superintendent will find it easy to generate enthusiasm for mission. This will be almost as true for mission in the United States and Canada as it is for mission in other world areas. In fact, there is some evidence that the younger generation prefers mission at home to mission elsewhere.

16. Promote sponsorship at the annual home mission service.

An annual home mission service at the district assembly is a preferred time and method for generating excitement for starting new churches. Showcasing the progress of recent NewStarts and revealing plans for more new beginnings is a proven effective method. A challenging message from the general superintendent or other new-church advocate strongly contributes to the service's impact. Keith Wright's home mission service on the Kansas City District is the biggest extravaganza of the year! Videos, skits, and a variety of visuals are helpful in making the service special and exciting. It is a good time to ask for special support for district home mission projects. Many districts renew their home mission club pledges at this service.

17. Keep the promotion going all year long.

To keep the excitement going throughout the year, regular promotion in publications and at district gatherings is important. People easily determine what is important to a leader by what he or she talks most about. If a district superintendent mentions new churches every time he or she speaks and if this is done with enthusiasm, people will know that starting new churches is really important to the leader.

18. Promotional ideas abound.

Providing seminars and conferences on the topic of starting new churches will also build excitement for mission. Bringing in specialists and motivational speakers adds flair and gives variety to the cause. Logos, giveaways, theme songs, web sites, contests, banquets, brochures, skits, and many other items are routinely used to create excitement for mission on the district.

19. One district raised home mission funds through the NYI.

In the 1950s and 1960s, before the division of the old Northern California District, the NYI (formerly NYPS) used to have an annual banquet at which they raised money to start new churches. It was one of the most exciting events on the district. Each church would come to the banquet prepared to announce their contribution to home missions in the coming year. Excitement mounted the entire evening as anticipation embraced reality when the pledges were tallied. Creating excitement for mission turns a task into a glory.

20. Securing the right leader is the key to the success of a NewStart.

The most important, and often the most difficult, part of starting a new church is securing an appropriate leader. The ultimate success of the project depends largely on the leader. If everything is just right for starting the new church but the wrong leader is selected, the project is likely to falter or fail. With an appropriate leader, even a difficult situation may succeed beyond all expectations. For these reasons, the New-Start strategy provides Assessment Centers to help identify leaders with the qualities necessary to lead a new church.

21. Assessment Centers.

Assessment Centers are conducted at various times and locations. They typically last four days to provide ample observation by multiple trained assessors. Candidates are evaluated on the basis of criteria established through past observation. While the process is not an exact science, it does provide a filter for giving some indication of the ability of a person to lead a new church start-up. A favorable assessment often gives confidence to a person who senses a call to start a new church. That was just the encouragement Chris and Stephanie Carpenter needed to go start the Boise Euclid Community Church on the Intermountain District.

22. The College of New Church Knowledge.

The NewStart strategy also provides the College of New Church Knowledge. This is not just another seminar on how to start a new church. The distinctive characteristic of this event is training in entrepreneurship. We looked all over America before we learned that Babson College in Boston was the leading school in entrepreneurship training. We have adapted the principles of entrepreneurship for NewStart ventures. A new-church leader must be able to accomplish a goal with limited resources. Such a leader has an entrepreneurial-type personality, but certain principles of entrepreneurship can be learned. The College of New Church Knowledge focuses on teaching those principles.

23. There is value in being a denominational church.

The College of New Church Knowledge also includes direction in beginning a denominationally connected church. While a variety of kinds and styles of churches is accepted, the College does not favor independent churches. The approach is to help the potential leader understand the benefits of being connected within a network of churches. The research coming out of *Faith Communities Today (FACT)* has revealed much greater denominational commitment than has been assumed by many.

24. You can get an adequate overview of how to start a new church.

A third aspect of the College of New Church Knowledge is training in the basics of starting a new church. It is not a detailed process but an adequate overview. There are several seminars available from various organizations that provide training in great depth for beginning a new church. These are recommended where time and funding permit participation.

25. The logical leader may not be the right leader.

Sometimes a church, contemplating sponsoring a new church, has a person in their membership who appears to be a likely choice to lead the new project. This person is usually well regarded in the local fellowship and is considered ideal for the assignment. Unfortunately, such a person often lacks the required traits and abilities to be an effective leader of a new church. This creates a potentially conflictive situation between the sponsoring pastor and the district superintendent.

26. Bring knowledge and desire together.

Obviously, the district superintendent has *Manual* authority and must approve the person who will be designated pastor of the new congregation. A district superintendent is experienced in making pastoral arrangements and knows more about the placement of pastors than most other people. On the other hand, the sponsoring church may be investing heavily in the project and may want to select a leader they believe will ensure the success of the project. One of the erroneous assumptions of some people in the local church is that district superintendents place pastors out of convenience and without regard to the needs of the situation. This is certainly not the case, because the district superintendent has as much, or more, to lose in an unsuccessful placement as anyone involved. But the district superintendent must accept the misperception and work with the pastor to choose the right person. Sending the sponsoring church's candidate to an Assessment Center can be a productive way of dealing with the situation.

27. Show me first your penny. Indeed, I have not any.

A more common situation is the lack of any candidate for leadership of the new project. We are frequently asked for recommendations of pastors capable of starting new churches. There may be pastors on the district who want to move. There may be unassigned ordained elders on the district who would like to be given a church. The district superintendent's file may be full of résumés from clergypersons all across the country. Yet for many reasons no appropriate candidate can be identified. In such cases, often overlooked leaders are already on site.

28. Don't overlook gifted and highly capable lay leaders.

Highly capable lay leaders sometimes make outstanding leaders of new congregations. They may have the needed leadership ability, entrepreneurial skills, winsome personality, teaching experience, and strong Christian character and unquestioned commitment to the church—both the Kingdom and the denomination. This was the situation in Mount Jefferson, North Carolina, where we convinced the late Gilbert Dancy, a retired Chrysler executive, to be the initial leader for the new church. The NewStart strategy provides special training resources for laypersons chosen to be the leaders of new churches.

29. Give serious consideration to women clergy as new-church leaders.

Women clergy are another source of leaders for new churches. There are significant numbers of women receiving a call to preach and pursuing studies in seminary. Many have already completed their ministerial preparation but have not yet been given an assignment. The abilities required to form a new congregation are often native to women. Their intuition, compassion, and persistence serve them well in forming a new faith community. Yet it is advisable to send women candidates to Assessment Centers to determine their appropriateness for starting new churches.

30. The plan worked, but we hated it.

In the late 1970s and early 1980s, it was common to hear new-church advocates declare you could start a new church without any people or money. Many churches were started that way, and today many of them are solid churches. Dr. Neil Wiseman, editor of *GROW* magazine, reported on the Oregon Plan 10 years after it happened and found 27 churches still in existence and several of them to be solid congregations. But the perception of the church is that that strategy was a fiasco. This perception is untrue, but you can't keep people from believing what they want to believe.

31. The NewStart strategy is built on research.

The NewStart strategy is built on a different concept. In one sense, it is a response to the perception of people. But in the true sense, it is built on careful research. At the end of the 1980s, Dale Jones of the Church Growth Research Center at Nazarene Headquarters made a study of all the new churches started during the decade. He discovered that out of all the new churches, only 7 percent had grown to a membership over 85 after four years of existence. He followed up on the research and contacted the districts where the 7 percent of stronger churches were located. He inquired about the way those churches were started. Three common characteristics were discovered. First, all of the stronger churches began with a core group of Nazarenes. Second, they all had some financial support, usually described as "adequate." Third, they each had a new-church leader experienced in ministry. The New-Start strategy—created by district superintendents—of "starting strong new churches the right way" drew heavily from this research.

32. When it comes to core groups, bigger is better.

The research recommended starting a new church with a core group of Nazarenes to give direction and stability to the new congregation. The size of the group may vary depending on the situation, but as a general rule, the bigger the better. The research also revealed that new churches with a core group of 40 or more did significantly better than those with less than 40. Not only was the survival rate better, but also long-term growth was greater.

33. A new church typically has a four-year window of opportunity.

Growth usually plateaus after the first four years, regardless of the circumstances under which a new church is started. No obvious data explain this phenomenon. There are several theories, but the best insight is to make the most of the first four years. That is what I told a friend of mine who was in the third year of a NewStart—make the most of this year! There is sometimes the feeling that a new church has plenty of time to get going and established. It has no such luxury. Time is of the essence. Once the new congregation is founded, every effort should be put forth to develop it to the greatest extent possible. This raises the question of evaluation. How should it be determined whether or not the church is succeeding?

34. It is important to evaluate the progress of the NewStart.

Attendance is the No. 1 criteria. This is not popular, but it is reliable. Counting people present each Sunday will indicate if new people are being brought into the fellowship. New churches exist and thrive on new converts. A new group may report many worthwhile ministries and activities, but unless they also report new converts and increasing attendance, it is in need of attention. Unfortunately, this may be the first glimmer of insight that the wrong leader has been chosen. Of course, immediately jumping to that conclusion is unwise. There may be other problems. Besides, you are probably stuck with the leader you have. So it is better to study the situation and work to improve problem areas. For example, the meeting place may be the problem. If so, help them find a new location. Or the problem may be that the core group has unrealistic expectations of new people. Instruct the leader how to get the members to ease their demands on new people. If it becomes apparent the leader is just not winning people, then assigning a coach to improve a specific deficiency might be an excellent investment.

35. There is no set time for official organization to occur.

At what point in time a new congregation should be officially organized is a matter of question. As a district superintendent, I pushed new start-ups to organize quickly so I could report it to Kansas City! I wouldn't do that today. The NewStart strategy specifies that a new church should not be fully organized until it is self-supporting. This is based on the "New Church Sponsor Agreement" negotiated between the sponsor and the district at the beginning of the project. On the other hand, some new-church specialists believe delaying organization is counterproductive. They insist organization produces a distinct identity that encourages growth and development.

36. Don't force or prevent organization.

It is probably a mistake to force a group to prematurely organize. Likewise, it is probably unwise to prevent a congregation from organizing when they truly desire that recognition. There is no denominational benefit or district advantage in early organization—as once was the case. Making that determination is an occasion for exercising the partnership between the district and the sponsoring church.

37. Just do it!

There is no ritual in the *Manual* for organizing a new church. In fact, there are no criteria for organization at all. A district superintendent can organize practically anything he or she wants to. There is no form to sign, no document to file, no account to activate. It is simply as the Nike ad says, "Just Do It."

38. Make it a celebration because it is really a Kingdom event.

Even so, making organization a significant event in the life of the church adds to the identity of the church and helps bond them to the district organization. Organization day is a day of fulfillment. What was once only a vision has become a reality. The risk and adventure have demonstrated the power of the gospel. The sacrifice and commitment have returned a joy beyond expression. Another community of faith in the kingdom of God has been established. God's kingdom is indeed at hand!

39. A district superintendent's job is spiritual too!

God has called you to win people to Christ and help build His kingdom. The church has never discovered a method of evangelism more effective than starting new churches. A district superintendent is in the unique position of encouraging the starting of many new churches. Like pastors exhorting their laity to witness, district superintendents encourage their churches to sponsor new churches. A district superintendent can count hundreds, even thousands, of people who have come to Christ and the church as the result of his or her encouragement to start new churches. A missional district is an evangelistic powerhouse. What an assignment, what a glory—being entrusted and challenged to develop a missional district.

▷ ▷ ▷

"Multiple churches
serve as multiple
points of entry
into the
kingdom of God."
—Bill M. Sullivan

▷ ▷ ▷

Your Church Can Start a New Church

Everyone Can Do Something

NEIL B. WISEMAN

FIVE OR SIX PASTORS sat talking shop around the fireplace at the winter pastors' retreat. It was a casual conversation, but Jim spoke with a pensive mood: "I keep wondering how the apostle Paul's testimony serves as a pattern for my work."

"What testimony is that?" asked Scott.

Jim answered, "You know, the passage our resource leader used in her message last night. I mean those 'all' words in Paul's sentence, 'I am made *all* things to *all* men, that I might by *all* means save some'" (1 Cor. 9:22, KJV, emphases added).

He continued, "It seems so big—so inclusive, so extensive, so kind of universal—enormous and almost ultimate. It just doesn't fit my congregation of 95. I have trouble getting ahold of it. All things. All people. Save some."

Ivan spoke up, "Yeah, I have trouble with that passage too. My trouble is caused by the notion we so often hear, 'I am not called to get results but to be faithful.' What happens if faithful does not accomplish the 'all things' Paul had in mind?"

Mindy offered a fresh insight: "I can do something, though I can't do everything. I can win one as a start on winning the world."

Jim said, "I think about the concept in relationship to our church in a town of 15,000, 85 miles from a big city. Being a Kingdom outpost that is charged by the Great Commission to evangelize every person makes me wonder how that can be done."

The veteran pastor of 40 years, Michael, said, "In quiet moments of soul searching, every Christian leader—pastor or lay leader—realizes that a particular church will not attract every people group for whom that church bears spiritual responsibility."

Jim replied, "That's my point—how can we do it? My heart longs to start a new church, even though we have only 83 members. Is it possible? Dare we try?"

COULD OUR CHURCH START A CHURCH?— THE QUESTION EVERY PASTOR SOMETIMES ASKS

Let's break away from the pastors' meeting to do some hard thinking on our own. Let's ask the question every pastor sometimes asks, "Could I start a new church as part of my call to win as many people as possible to Christ?"

First things first. Rid yourself of those suspicions that starting a new church will hinder your church—it won't. Strange as it seems, new churches help existing churches rather than hinder them.

Diversity among those we seek to win to Christ—like the unchurched from established populations and our new neighbors from around the world—requires that we speak so needy people understand us. Sometimes a congregation's first reaction to diversity is to think their church can set the spiritual table and let others come if they want to eat. The idea is that they can adjust to the way we do it; they can take us or leave us.

But leading people to faith never works that way. Missionaries always cross the distance of language and culture. Missionaries are never sent to Peru who say to prospects, "Either learn English or forget the possibilities of the gospel." No, no. The "sent ones" learn the language and study the culture so "those to whom they are sent" can be introduced to Christ in their own language.

Another communication difficulty also exists in the secular social climates of the United States and Canada. In these settings, the language problem is not Spanish or German. Rather, it more likely is a problem involving the language of those who give their whole attention to material values—something like what the apostle Paul faced at Mars Hill when he spoke to the Athenians about their "UNKNOWN GOD" (see Acts 17, KJV). You remember. He started with what they valued so he could get them to really listen to what he wanted them to hear.

GETTING ACQUAINTED WITH NEWSTART

NewStart, an easily remembered name, describes a new-church evangelism movement that is greatly impacting the Church of the Nazarene. In fact, NewStart has made new-church evangelism a priority in our denomination.

NewStart, a contemporary strategy for starting strong new churches, enables local congregations to start churches as the highly effective method of evangelism.

NewStart helps congregations and local church leaders realize that nearby unchurched areas are as important to God as overseas missions.

NewStart provides information and training that helps church starters and core groups avoid costly mistakes others made in the past.

NewStart, a throughly researched and carefully planned methodology, helps a local congregation be willing to leave its comfort zone.

NewStart is a strategy for starting new churches that has been shaped by district superintendents and contains the components they thought best to include. In the summer of 1995, Dr. Bill M. Sullivan led sessions of extensive discussions about how best to multiply starting churches with all United States district superintendents. Those sessions were held at each PALCON session on the college and university campuses. Later that year, the program received full approval of the Board of General Superintendents.

NewStart is the renewal of a strategy used in the earlier years of our denominational history. In those days, pastors, evangelists, laypersons, and congregations all started new churches and districts that organized the fruits of their labors. Holding home mission revivals with the intention of organizing a church at the end of the campaign was common; pastors, evangelists, and district superintendents often gave themselves to this task as part of their calling. Our forebears believed their work was not done until every community had a Holiness church.

NEWSTART STANDS ON FOUR STURDY CORNERSTONES

NewStart builds on four cornerstones. Let's consider the rationale for each one of them.

Cornerstone No. 1—New churches are the most effective method of evangelism.

The unchurched are not likely to beg the church for a gospel witness in their community. In fact, many spiritually needy individuals do not realize what they need. So if we are to win the unchurched to Jesus and develop them into disciples, we will have to go to them.

The question then becomes, "How do we know starting new churches is the most effective method of evangelism?" Several significant answers must be considered:

• New churches win more people because they are focused on outreach.

• New churches win more people because they usually pray more and often have wide prayer support from established churches.

• New churches win more people because they attract adventuresome folks who want to be in on the ground floor of a new work for God.

• New churches win more people because they require a high level of involvement from everyone.

• New churches win more people because they are typically started among receptive people groups.

• New churches, according to several research studies, win more converts per member and dollar than established churches.

• New churches win more people because they are free to try new methods and strategies; no traditions have been set in concrete.

• New churches win more people because they are usually more responsive to new people than older, established churches.

Cornerstone No. 2—New-church evangelism is motivated by missional commitments.

Nazarenes have a glorious history of investing heart, brain, brawn, devotion, prayers, and money in any cause that brings Christ to new people. Our denomination, congregations, and individual members are mission minded and mission hearted.

Nazarenes believe the New Testament ties holiness and missional responsibilities together—Acts 1:8 is one example. As a result, pastors and lay leaders can expect that Nazarenes will willingly engage in missional efforts across the United States and Canada if they are shown a process that elicits their confidence and involvement. NewStart is that plan.

Starting new churches is the "sleeping giant" of evangelism today, especially for Nazarenes. Our 10,000 clergy and 600,000 laypersons in North America represent an incredible force for spreading the Good News. We must awaken this giant—start churches, win hundreds of thousands of new people, and strengthen our own souls with the spiritual calisthenics new-church evangelism requires.

Starting strong new churches is a gift we give God and a gift we give our unsaved neighbors. But it is also a rich gift we give our congregations.

Consider these benefits.

• Missional pastors see themselves as Kingdom servants rather than mere maintenance leaders.

• Missional pastors, in starting new churches as pastor or sponsoring pastor, experience a rekindling of their call to win lost people.

• Missional pastors, as they deal with the opportunities around them, are challenged to look past the missionary myth that missionary efforts have to be done across an ocean. NewStart brings missions home.

• Missional pastors realize that secularization demands that new-church evangelism reach across culture and values.

• The missional challenge calls every pastor and church in the United States and Canada to replicate the intensity and sacrifice they invest in overseas missions.

• Becoming missional heals a church from spiritual hypochondria as it focuses on others.

Since starting new churches offers so many benefits, why not get started now?

Cornerstone No. 3—New-church evangelism calls for starting strong new churches the right way.

Total dependence upon God, coupled with our best efforts, is our only hope for maximizing the NewStart strategies. Veteran missional leader David J. Hesselgrave summarizes what we all know to be true: "The accomplishment of God's plans and purpose requires divine wisdom, intervention, and grace. But it also requires that a Moses and his elders, or a Paul and his companions, dedicate themselves—body, heart, and mind—to the task."[1]

Since God wants our neighbors saved, He wants His Church to develop plans and call Christians to strategies that are biblically sound and effective. He wants plans that will inspire His people to be involved, even to sacrifice.

Hesselgrave says of the apostle Paul, "Under God, Paul was at the forefront of the campaign. . . . it seems obvious that the early missionary (developing new church) enterprise was characterized by discipline and direction."[2] It has to be true for us too. Discipline, direction, order, and workable plans are the starting points of new-church evangelism.

Too often the people of God have been asked to commit to a cause, such as starting churches, without a proven plan. Then when they do not respond, the leader calls it apathy and preoccupation. Let the challenge be to use NewStart to accomplish achievement for the Lord.

What are the factors in NewStart that will help us start strong new churches the right way?

• We must start with the motive of evangelism.

• We must start with a core group of willing people.

• We must have sufficient financial support to secure and maintain quality pastoral leadership.

• We must have pastors who are qualified to start churches.

• We must have a support network, like a sponsoring congregation, to assist in the first few years of its operation. The assessment program and process also helps achieve this purpose.

Cornerstone No. 4—New-church evangelism is best accomplished by local churches.

Local church sponsorship is a key component of the NewStart strategy. At the heart of this whole quest for new-church evangelism, our purpose is to reach the world for Christ—and we all know that districts and denominations cannot make that happen in an ultimate sense. Only local churches possess what is most needed—they pray, they give, and they encourage people to answer a call to serve. It is local congregations that can best birth a church, care for the baby, and nurture the new converts. And it is most effective to stimulate the established church with the Nazarene missional spirit for the new work when a fired-up pastor shares his or her burden with the people.

Consider this reality—wherever responsibility is placed for initiating new-church starts, local churches must ultimately provide the three elements necessary to effectively start any new church: financial assistance, a core group, and emotional support by their people.

It only makes sense that when "ownership" for starting new churches is handed to the local church, it will provide those three elements more effectively. In a nutshell, the local church is in the best position to initiate a new-church start because of these things:

• **Proximity**. A sponsoring church can stay close to the fledgling congregation, providing spiritual and emotional support. A steering committee from the sponsoring church, for example, can invest much more time in the new church than a district-appointed committee that might be scattered among several churches and over hundreds of additional miles.

• **Finances and Other Resources.** A sponsoring church can generate financial support in a variety of ways, whereas district resources are primarily budgetary. When the members of a sponsoring church really get behind a new start, they become a major source of multiplied "soft dollars." They make sure that their "baby" is properly cared for. Soft dollars include cash gifts (outside the normal budget), gifts-in-kind, discounted purchases, volunteer labor, donated services and equipment, and much more.

• **More People Getting Involved in Ministry**. Local church sponsorship gives church members hands-on involvement in mission. This brings excitement and satisfaction to the sponsoring church constituency.

The local church can better serve as the principal source of the new-church core group if it assumes ownership for starting the new church. Then, rather than feeling defeated because they are losing members, the pastor and laity of the sponsoring church get to feel the victory of giving from a sense of abundance.

• **Better Targeting.** Sponsorship also allows the local church to define "the right way" to start a new church. Since the local church is closer to those areas needing new churches, its people are better able to understand the local contextual factors that will influence the development of a new church. Thus the selection of new-church targets by existing churches will be better focused.

• **Local Control.** The local church has control of the entire project. It even has the right to choose the pastor of the new congregation—with two important provisions: (1) The district superintendent must approve the pastor of any church, new or old, large or small, and (2) the sponsoring church cannot return a non-self-supporting project to the district. The sponsoring church selects in which town/community the church will be started, when it will begin, and when it will be fully organized.

• **Full Satisfaction of Joy.** The local church has full rights to rejoice in seeing (1) new people come to know Christ, (2) a new congregation formed, and (3) the kingdom of God extended to a new community.

WAYS SMALLER CHURCHES CAN SPONSOR NEW WORKS

There are a variety of sponsorship plans depending on the needs of the church a local congregation plans to start and depending on the resources of the local church. A plan is an organized way that allows each church and each pastor to be significantly involved. Here are several viable options:

1. A "Single Church" sponsorship provides most of the prayer power, the emotional support, and the contact personnel for a bivocational new-church starter. (The new church may be a multicultural congregation; an English-speaking, white congregation; or an integrated congregation.) In this plan, the sponsoring church might not provide any of the core group and very little money (perhaps only their home mission budget money that the district directs to the new

church). They would, of course, be able to provide some "soft-dollar" support (poundings for the new-church starter family, surplus furniture and equipment, etc.). Their greatest contribution would be to provide contact personnel who could perform activities such as telephoning, mailing advertisements, distributing handbills, making personal contacts, and so on. Perhaps equally important would be prayer and emotional support for the entire project. Naturally, many of these churches would be able to provide office space (and perhaps some volunteer service) for the new-church start. In some cases, their church building might be used for Bible study and other groups.

2. "Joint" sponsorship in cooperation with one or a few other churches provides some (or all) of the support for the new-church starter. Each church might provide one or more families for the core group—or they might not contribute anyone to the core group.

3. "Zone" sponsorship (all of the churches on a district zone) could provide full financial support of a new-church project and, in some cases, an adequate core group. In this instance, there is a good opportunity to build the core group from the "outside in" instead from the "inside out." This means, having full financial support, the new-church starter could concentrate on reaching new people in the new community—although our experience indicates new churches thrive on well-trained leaders.

4. "Pairing" sponsorship (90/10 or 80/20) combines a small and a large church together to begin a new church in a community from which both sponsoring churches draw attenders or for some other mutual interest. The small church might contribute only 10 or 20 percent of the funding necessary for the support of a full-time new-church starter and a similar percentage of the core group.

5. "District Teaming" sponsorship joins a small local church with the district to begin a new church the district believes the community needs and is willing to help sponsor. In most instances, though not always, this will be a multicultural church. The district may provide funding but depend on the local church to provide the use of their building, emotional support of the new-church leader, volunteer helpers, soft-dollar support of the project, and so on.

6. "Replacement" sponsorship is the action of a small and declining congregation to perpetuate a Holiness ministry in their city. It accepts several realities:

   a. Although their church was well situated 25 or 30 years ago, it is no longer in a favorable location to reach new young families.

b. The average age of the membership is increasing as the attendance decreases.

c. The congregation chooses, instead of relocating, to remain in the present community as a continuing witness to the people of that community.

d. The present congregation has the power to "prevent or allow" a new church to be started in a new section of their town. Such a church can decide to make it possible for a new, young, vibrant, and culturally relevant church to be started in a favorable location. They can provide various kinds of support—but the most significant one will be the decision to allow a new congregation to be started!

7. "Testamentary" sponsorship involves the commitment of a congregation that upon the disorganization of their church all the remaining assets will be invested in a new church in their town. It would also provide for a savings account to be established, into which they might contribute funds, for the future support of starting a new church in their town.

8. "Creative Plan" sponsorship allows for customizing to fit the sponsoring church/churches and the new congregation. As people pray about the needs and possibilities, the Holy Spirit may lead in ways not previously envisioned. Churches engaged in mission will see the best options and select the best methods.

DETAILS FOR CHURCHES WHO DO FULL SPONSORSHIPS

Full sponsorship empowers an existing local church with several options.

1. Focus—to select the general area where the new church will be located and the particular target group to which the church will minister.

2. Timetable—to determine the timetable, within reasonable limits, for the development and organization of the new church. Past experience indicates that a new church will reach its potential in its first four years of operation.

3. Reporting statistics—to include the attendance and membership of the new church within the official records and reports of the sponsoring church until the new church is officially and fully organized. Outside of the official records and reports, every effort must be made to publicize the progress of the new church. News stories in dis-

trict papers are preferable to statistical reports. In news stories, both the new church and the sponsoring church can be properly affirmed. Recognition can also be given to the district for new district sponsorships. The present plan of recognizing only fully organized churches has to change.

4. Choosing the pastor—to select, in consultation with the district superintendent, the person who will become the pastor of the new church.

Since the pastor is essential to the success of the church, every effort should be exerted to choose a person who has been formally assessed and certified as a church starter. The right to select the new-church pastor must be the prerogative of the sponsoring church. However, the pastor of the sponsoring church should take advantage of the district superintendent's training and extensive experience in the selection of personnel. The superintendent will always be an important resource person in choosing a new-church starter.

The most important decision that will be made regarding the starting of a new church is the selection of the founding pastor. Special gifts are necessary to be an effective pastor of a new church. For this reason, a careful process of selection is essential.

The assessment retreats are designed to help determine whether a potential pastor and spouse have the gifts and graces to start a new church. At those retreats, interviewing and observing potential new-church pastors takes place. All methods of evaluation are utilized during the event: résumés, recommendations, interviews, testing, profiling, simulations, performance, and general observation. A careful distinction is drawn between a person's call to ministry and his or her ability to be the founding pastor of a new church. At the end of the event, each couple/person is rated (1) approved, (2) may reapply after two years, or (3) not approved.

Assessment retreats have been extensively used for several years with demonstrated effectiveness. Some denominations report dramatic improvements in successful new-church starts as a result of using assessment retreats.

Churches that decide to fully sponsor a new church may choose to initially employ a staff person with the objective of having that person become the pastor of the new church. It is advisable to engage a person who has been certified as a church starter by an Assessment Center.

For a year or two, the staff person could serve in a dual role of regular staff person and future pastor, working toward the beginning of the new church.

5. Budgets—to receive the return of the District Home Mission Budget or negotiate with the district superintendent the return of a percentage of the budget, for example, 50 to 75 percent. The various circumstances of particular districts will help determine the percentage of budget returned to sponsoring churches. The budget return agreement will include budget money paid to the district within each assembly year that the new church is sponsored, up to a maximum of four full years, provided such cash funds are actually invested in the new church.

6. Exemption—to have all cash (or a significant portion) invested in the new church reported in "Column 11*b*," which means it will be exempt from budgets.

7. Ten percent credit—to receive 10 Percent Giving Credit for all cash invested in the new church within each assembly year.

Full sponsorship carries certain obligations.

1. Excellence—a commitment to excellence in starting the new church. The goal is a strong new church, fully organized and fully self-supporting.

2. Leadership—a willingness to permanently give leadership and other personnel to form the core group of the new church.

3. Oversight—a willingness to provide continuing concern for and oversight of the new-church project until it is fully organized.

4. Certified leader—agreement to work closely with the district superintendent in the selection of a new-church pastor and to choose leadership that has been recommended to begin a new church by a certified Assessment Center.

5. Finance—a willingness to assume full financial responsibility for starting the new church and bringing it to fully organized status. The process, including financial commitments, should be developed and accomplished in consultation with the district superintendent and the District Advisory Board. Special care should be given to establishing the habit of budget payments. Perhaps the new church would volunteer to contribute to each budget of the sponsoring church, even though the district had not assigned the new church a budget. A graduated scale of budget responsibility should be instituted during the years that the new church is under the direction of the sponsoring church.

6. Self-support—agreement that the new church will not be returned to the district for responsibility until, and unless, the new

church is fully self-supporting. This includes responsibility for mortgages and all indebtedness.

IT'S TIME TO START

Why not ask the Lord today—right now—what He wants you and your church to do in this great effort.

One entry in the minutes of the First General Assembly, held in Chicago in 1907 and chaired by Dr. P. F. Bresee, explains the purpose of the Church of the Nazarene: "Nothing short of planting this work in every considerable city in this country, from which it may radiate to villages and country round about, and the doing it as soon as possible, will meet the necessities. Our Lord has called us to do this work. His own hand beckons us on. He opens the door, and it must be our business to enter this land of promise and possess it for Him and His glory."[3]

Did you hear the founder's instruction?

1. Focus—"radiate to villages and country."
2. Promptness—"as soon as possible."
3. "Necessities"—an essential task He wants done.
4. Call—God "called us to do this work."
5. Opportunity—"He opens the door."
6. Possess the land—claim it for the glory of our God.

And hear the promise of Scripture—"And surely I am with you always, to the very end of the age" (Matt. 28:20).

What Kind of a Church Do You Want to Start?

Making Our Brand Name Work for Us

KENNETH CROW

YOU NAZARENES KEEP YOUR FEET firmly planted on the doctrine and life of holiness." That advice came from a denominational outsider who walked unannounced into a Nazarene bull session. This was not just an opinionated outsider but Dr. Martin Marty, the renowned church historian, distinguished professor at the University of Chicago Divinity School, author of more than 40 books, and longtime *Christian Century* columnist.

But I am a little ahead of my story.

The occasion was a bull session where a group who loves God and the church were having a rousing debate about the church's future. This was not a gathering of fringe malcontents but a group of effective pastors, educators, and other leaders who have made many important contributions to the church. So the meeting was really a lovers' quarrel, and the debate was heated.

Earlier in the conference, Dr. Martin Marty had inspired us with a brilliant presentation. But he skipped this discussion session to respond to national news media types who telephoned to get his opinions about a major new survey about American religion. The survey showed that more than 100,000 Americans had been interviewed about their religious affiliation and the picture was much more positive than many expected. The media knew they had the raw material for an unusual story, and they wanted an expert's perspective.

Our group was having an insiders' argument—just us Nazarenes. Nazarenes are good at this kind of meeting, usually held informally during conferences or pastors' retreats. Someone used the apostle Paul's image that calls the Church a body and wondered aloud about our denominational body's health and aging process. Someone else resoundingly rejected the very idea of thinking about the Church as a living organism. We griped about our failings. We argued as we tried to pinpoint nonnegotiables. We raised identity issues. Everyone longed to see our church renewed, but we couldn't agree on how to do it. We were committed to the doctrine of holiness, but we did not agree about the best ways to take our rich heritage into the next generation and into the new century. Of course, there were questions about whether it helped or hindered to use the name "Nazarene."

When the discussion turned toward the holiness message, we suddenly heard Martin Marty's voice from the back of the room. He had finished with the media and slipped into the back of our meeting room. With passion he urged us to emphasize the doctrine of holiness. He reminded us that the people of his church, the Lutherans, plant their feet firmly on the doctrine of justification by faith. Without neglecting other doctrines, they emphasize this one—not only for their people but also for all Christians. "In the same way," he argued, "you Nazarenes plant your feet firmly on the doctrine of holiness." Without neglecting other doctrines, he urged that we emphasize the importance of Christlikeness as communicated in the holiness message. He insisted with amazing zeal that the rest of the Christian Church needs us to faithfully hold high the doctrine of holiness.

▷ ▷ ▷

Dr. Marty made us realize that the Church of the Nazarene is better than we insiders sometimes think—probably much better.

▷ ▷ ▷

Dr. Marty also challenged us to understand that renewal of the church could come by renewing our own commitments to our founder's commitments—commitments to be a thoroughly Christian church and to give special attention and voice to holiness. His bottom line was this—cherish and communicate the message, but always be ready to change your methods to fit the needs of the times.

That day Dr. Marty made us realize that the Church of the Nazarene is better than we insiders sometimes think—probably much better. Most of us insiders could use an unbiased observer now and then to remind us of our strengths.

Those who start new churches need to understand those strengths and build them into new works. They need to realize the advantages of highlighting our denominational connection over starting more independent, generic, evangelical churches.

BRAND NAMES VS. GENERIC LABELS

Several years ago, Americans went through a phase of choosing generic labels over brand names. Generic products became the rage because they usually cost less. The rationale was that bread by generic or brand name was still bread, milk was milk, peanut butter was peanut butter, and gasoline was gasoline. So why pay a higher price for a famous name?

At about the same time, some highly visible religious influencers and writers started to promote minimizing or dropping denominational labels completely, especially in new-church evangelism. The logic went like this—persons coming from other backgrounds might feel excluded if the name is prominent. Every denomination has some regrettable history. So why not be more inclusive and get rid of the negative baggage by playing down the connection. A neutral name, something such as "Community Fellowship," might be more attractive to new people. So in some geographic areas you find five "community churches" in a six- or eight-block radius.

In response to these ideas, Dale Jones, of the Nazarene Research Center, became professionally curious and conducted a study comparing new churches that chose to downplay the Nazarene connection in their name with those who chose to include the connection. He found little difference between the two. In practice, minimizing the Nazarene name was not a great advantage.

Faith Communities in the United States Today (FACT), the largest survey of congregations ever conducted in the United States, discovered that most congregations (62 percent) of all denominations clearly express their denominational heritage. Only 13 percent disagreed with the description that their congregation clearly expresses its denominational heritage. The expression of denominational heritage tends to be stronger in those congregations with a distinctive racial/ethnic/national identity. (The study was conducted from the fall of 1999 to the spring of 2000. Congregational leaders, usually the pastor, completed the questionnaire. Further information may be found on the project web site at <www.fact.hartsem.edu>.)

Richard Houseal of the Nazarene Research Center at the Kansas City International Center led our denomination's participation in the *FACT* survey. Among Nazarene congregations, 60 percent said they clearly express their Nazarene heritage. As in the overall study, only 13 percent of Nazarene congregations said this description was only slightly or not at all accurate.

Opponents of affirming the denominational connection might, however, argue that the 60 percent are the spiritually dead congregations. Not so! In fact, 87 percent of the pastors who say their congregations clearly express their Nazarene heritage also say their congregations are spiritually vital and alive. In contrast, the congregations where denominational heritage is minimized are less likely to evaluate themselves as spiritually vital and alive. The research data is abundantly clear. Vital, healthy congregations emphasize their denominational heritage.

▷ ▷ ▷

The Nazarene "brand" represents historic Christianity with a special emphasis on the holy life.

▷ ▷ ▷

Now, let's revisit the generic issue in society. Time has passed. Americans have had more experience with generic labels and the products they represent. These days we may take a chance on minor generic items, but when the investment will be major, or the consequences great, we look for known qualities that brand names represent. When we shop for a car, we look for a manufacturer we trust.

These days a large part of the population of the Western world makes major decisions about electronic equipment, automobiles, clothing, and even breakfast cereal based on brand names. Brand names, such as Toshiba, Sony, Cadillac, McDonald's, Lexus, Bose, Kellogg's, and Wendy's, draw us to certain specific purchases.

To put the issue somewhat comically, does it not seem difficult to imagine a Wendy's restaurant posting a sign that reads "Community Fellowship Hamburgers"? Or a Cadillac car agency calling itself "the no name auto dealer"?

Indeed, companies that try to avoid brand connections are advised by two specialists that "any company that tried to get by with unconnected and directionless local brand strategies will inevitably find mediocrity as its reward."[1] The Nazarene "brand" represents historic Christianity with a special emphasis on the holy life. At its best, the Church of the Nazarene represents what millions of spiritually starved Americans are hungry for.

Let's squarely face the downside we sometimes hear associated with the Nazarene brand. The Church of the Nazarene is not always at its best, and we all regret that. But people don't stop choosing McDonald's because they once were served by a strange clerk—or stop going to Borders Book Stores because the manager had a bad day. Most businesses, like extended families, have a weird uncle and an eccentric aunt or two somewhere in their organization.

I love Karen Dean Fry's delightful story about how even peculiarity sometimes attracts people: "Papa was saved at 17 under the ministry of Brother Tidwell . . . [who] was very strict about a lot of things. I asked Papa if he believed the way Brother Tidwell did about coffee and neckties and other 'no-no's.' He smiled and said, 'I believed that those people loved me, and that felt a whole lot better than coffee ever tasted.'"[2]

The Nazarene name represents much too much to fully summarize it all here. But the Church of the Nazarene has a record of nearly a century of faithful commitment to seeking to live out the doctrine of holiness and to sharing its adventure with others. These days we are discovering even more effective ways to communicate our message and our discoveries by building three core values into everything we do in the church. In actual practice, these values are expressed in three missional ideals—these characteristics will help make any new church great.

STATED CORE VALUES HELP US KNOW WHO WE ARE

The recently published *Core Values: Church of the Nazarene*, developed and widely distributed by the Board of General Superintendents, states the core values and explains their purpose very well: "Every organization that endures over time is based on a deeply shared combination of purpose, belief, and values. So it is with the Church of the Nazarene. It was founded to transform the world by spreading scriptural holiness. It is both a Great Commission church and a Holiness church at the same time. Our mission is to make Christlike disciples of all nations."[3] Then the statement identifies three core values: (1) we are a Christian people, (2) we are a holiness people, and (3) we are a missional people.

1. The Church of the Nazarene is a Christian church.

The first core value states: "We are a Christian people. As members of the Church Universal, we join with all true believers in proclaiming the Lordship of Jesus Christ and in embracing the historic Trinitarian creedal statements of Christian faith. We value our Wesleyan-Holiness heritage and believe it to be a way of understanding the faith that is true to Scripture, reason, tradition, and experience."[4]

With all the people of God we confess and praise Jesus the Lord. We have experienced the divine love of God in forgiveness of sin. We have been reconciled to God and to each other. We love one another as we have been loved by God. We forgive each other as we have been forgiven by God.

Nazarenes are part of the unified, holy, universal, and apostolic Church. We affirm the essential beliefs of the Christian faith held by all Christians. Our special calling is to hold before the eyes of the world and the Church the centrality of holiness.

Dr. Paul G. Cunningham, general superintendent, emphasizes the reality that we are neither a cult nor a renegade church. Our articles of faith are shaped by the Bible and the ancient creeds of the Church.[5]

2. The Church of the Nazarene is a Holiness church.

"We are a Holiness people. God, who is holy, calls us to a life of holiness. We believe that the Holy Spirit seeks to do in us a second work of grace, called by various terms including 'entire sanctification' and 'baptism with the Holy Spirit'—cleansing us from all sin; renewing us in the image of God; empowering us to love God with our whole heart, soul, mind, and strength, and our neighbors as ourselves; and producing in us the character of Christ. Holiness in the life of believers is most clearly understood as Christlikeness."[6]

We identify with the Arminian tradition of free grace and human freedom. We trace our church heritage to the Wesleyan revival in the 18th century and to the Holiness Movement of the 19th and 20th centuries.

Dr. Jim L. Bond, general superintendent, explains the importance of this core value like this: "For 2000 years, Jesus has been the magnet of the church. He draws people to himself. They want to be near Him. They want to know Him better. And that magnetism draws people to any church where they think they will truly encounter the living Christ."[7]

3. The Church of the Nazarene is a missional church.

"We are a missional people. We are a 'sent people,' responding to the call of Christ and empowered by the Holy Spirit to go into all the world, witnessing to the Lordship of Christ and participating with God in the building of the Church and the extension of His kingdom (2 Corinthians 6:1). Our mission *(a)* begins in worship, *(b)* ministers to the world in evangelism and compassion, *(c)* encourages believers toward Christian maturity through discipleship, and *(d)* prepares women and men for Christian service through Christian higher education."[8]

As a missional people, we are committed to take the Great Commission in its fullest expression to the far corners of the earth as well as next door. In 1906, Phineas F. Bresee, founding Nazarene general superintendent, said: "Our church is preeminently a missionary church. It knows no difference between home and foreign fields—in these days all fields are near."[9] Though the word "missional" is new, its underpinning and practices have been a part of us from our earliest days. For Bresee, missions was not limited to other nations. It was global and local. And the same reality is present today.

MAKING MISSIONAL IDEALS OPERATIONAL IN OUR CHURCHES

Let's clarify what we mean by the term "missional." Nazarenes believe missional churches (1) make disciples of lost people, (2) commit to compassion evangelism, (3) reach across cultural barriers, and (4) reproduce themselves in new churches.

Here's how those characteristics are lived out among us.

▷ ▷ ▷

"Two factors—the changeless gospel and changeable methods—must shape our plans and fuel our strategies.

▷ ▷ ▷

A missional church makes disciples of lost people.

How is that done? How does that work in the local church? From the beginning, we have been a people's church seeking to lead people to Christ and to help them become productive disciples. Former General Superintendent William J. Prince offered this insight to help us accomplish the task of making disciples: "Two factors—the changeless gospel and changeable methods—must shape our plans and fuel our strategies as we seek to become more and more missional."[10]

• **Nazarenes welcome all people.** Nazarenes believe that God can transform anyone. They welcome the amazing variety of people God is drawing to himself. They really believe the transforming grace of God can redeem anyone.

One of our biblical patterns is the church at Philippi started by the apostle Paul. His first congregation had three key members who demonstrated amazing diversity—Lydia, a dealer in purple cloth; a slave girl formerly possessed with an evil spirit; and the local jailer, along with their households (Acts 16:11-40). In fact, Nazarenes have always welcomed the poor and the wealthy, the illiterate and the educated, the young as well as the old. "Our mission is not necessarily to enter the ranks of the prestigious, but to carry out the call of God ministering to *all* who are in need."[11]

Although we may not be as diverse as the Philippian church, a profile of Nazarenes in the United States shows that we represent a broad cross section of Americans. This was supported by a national survey of 113,000 American adults who were asked, "What is your religion?" and then they were asked several questions about their personal characteristics. The people who identified themselves in this study as Nazarene were a very diverse group, as we shall see in the next several characteristics.

• **Nazarenes enjoy an intergenerational family in most congregations.** Overall, we may be a little younger than the wider population. Only about 9 percent of the Nazarenes were older than 65 years compared to 20 percent of the overall population. We were very similar in the generation X age-group (18 to 25 at the time of the survey), with 16 percent compared to 17 percent overall. We had a larger proportion than the larger population in both the 26-to-45 and the 46-to-65 categories. We appear to be carrying on our mission to evangelize the young as well as the old.

• **Nazarenes welcome persons from all educational levels.** Nazarenes range in education from less than high school (20 percent) to graduate school (4 percent). In spite of an impressive network of colleges, most adult members have not attended college. High school graduation is the highest level of formal education completed for 57 percent of adult Americans and 65 percent of the Nazarenes. We have a strong commitment to higher education. However, the research shows our churches welcome people who are not highly educated.

• **Nazarenes welcome persons of all income levels.** The Nazarene household income distribution is similar to the national distribution. If there is a bias, it appears that we have been more successful in ministry to lower income groups. Almost half (48 percent) of the adult Nazarenes appear to have had total annual incomes of under $25,000. This is a higher proportion than found in the total population (42 percent). About 14 percent of the Nazarenes and of the larger population reported incomes below $10,000. Only 6 percent of Nazarenes, compared with 15 percent overall, had annual incomes greater than $50,000.

A missional church reaches across cultural barriers.

In a time like ours when the world has become a global village and migrants by the thousands are moving to our communities, the church has a grand opportunity to demonstrate the inclusive qualities of the gospel. Our progress is celebrated with a couple of sentences by General Superintendent Jerry D. Porter: "The Lord is shaping the Church of the Nazarene into a church for all people, all colors, all languages. We are becoming an inclusive church, with no second-class people, all receiving the fullness of the Holy Spirit, all pulling together, all impacting our world."[12]

• **Nazarenes support world missions.** The Church of the Nazarene believes in crossing cultural barriers with the gospel. We support hundreds of missionaries in 138 world areas and have become one of the largest missionary-sending agencies in the world.

• **Nazarenes are increasingly starting cross-cultural churches in the United States.** The churches in the United States must rise to the challenge of effectiveness in crossing nearby cultural barriers. There are currently 22 different cultural groups represented as the predominant groups in Nazarene churches in the United States. Of the 4,772 active, organized churches in 1999, 88 percent were white/English speaking. This is an improvement from 1990 when this percentage was 92 percent.

If these distributions of congregations are projected to the number of worshipers on an average Sunday morning, the 1990 proportion was 94 percent compared to 91 percent in 1999. To put this in perspective, it is important to know that in 1990 the overall U.S. population of white/non-Hispanics was 76 percent and in 1999 it was 72 percent. Although we are slowly becoming more diverse, this comparison to the population suggests that we still have a long way to go in our efforts to effectively disciple all the "nations" within our nation.

• **Nazarenes are starting new multicultural churches.** An increasing percentage of the newly organized Nazarene churches in the United States are multicultural. Established congregations are sharing their facilities. Pastors are migrating to the United States and Canada to serve these new churches. Immigrants are moving into most neighborhoods; some are even migrating to towns in the heartlands.

Over the past 20 years, 42 percent of the new churches have been other than English-speaking white. During the 1990s, this figure was 50 percent. In fact, in 4 of the last 5 years, there have been more multicultural churches organized than there have been white/English-speaking churches.

Dr. Tom Nees, Nazarene director of Mission Strategy USA/Canada, describes the present impressive developments favoring the establishment of multicultural churches: "Our global effectiveness is well known. Our missionaries have been wonderfully effective in other world areas. Many immigrants entering our countries are Nazarenes, both leaders and laypeople, who found the Lord and became a part of the international church in their homelands. Now they bring excitement and commitment for evangelism and church planting to the North American church."[13]

A missional church commits to compassion evangelism.

Nazarenes believe holiness and compassion belong together. Dr. Ron Benefiel, president of Nazarene Theological Seminary, quotes an insightful comment from District Superintendent Clarence Kinzler: "Compassionate ministries come naturally for us. Way down deep, it's part of who we are. It's in our bones." Benefiel continues with a challenge to us to be "a movement of Holiness people who are radically and fully committed to God, to one another, and to the mission of the church. . . . A people who take both the Great Commission and the Great Commandment seriously. The Church of the Nazarene—a people of evangelism, compassion, justice. *It's in our bones!*"[14] Compassion is an important part of what it means to be a Holiness people. And that compassion is always being expressed in hundreds, maybe thousands, of individual ways. Nazarenes offer needy people the ministry of compassion because that is what Jesus did. The evangelism aspect of compassion evangelism grows out of persons wanting to know why we offer compassion.

• **Nazarenes are committed to caring compassion.** Nazarene congregations find a variety of ways to help needy people. They develop programs on their own and in cooperation with other congregations, agencies, or organizations. The *FACT* survey, mentioned earlier in this chapter, showed most Nazarene congregations involved in some form of compassionate ministry for their own people or for people in the community.

• **Nazarenes respond to economic needs.** The most common form of service provided in the last 12 months was cash assistance to families or individuals. Almost all (96 percent) of the congregations provided this kind of assistance. Nearly as many (84 percent) provided, or helped to provide, a food pantry or soup kitchen. A majority (56 percent) provided a thrift store or thrift store donations.

• **Nazarenes care for physical and emotional needs.** Forty-four percent of our congregations provided services in hospitals or nursing homes during the last 12 months. About one-third provided or participated in a prison or jail ministry (34 percent), senior citizen programs other than housing (33 percent), and counseling services or a hot line (32 percent).

A missional church reproduces itself in new churches.

In calling the denomination to start strong new churches the right way, Dr. Bill M. Sullivan takes us back to basics: "It must be understood that the only purpose for this new strategy [NewStart] is to win people to Jesus Christ. It is not a plan to expand the denomination or even to grow the local church. It is simply an effort to utilize the most effective method of winning people to Christ. . . . He [Jesus] builds His Church. We are His servants and seek only to please Him. He has given us specific instructions about taking the Good News to the entire world—beginning in our local cities. Since this is God's will, we believe He will help us develop a plan that will inspire His people to become involved."[15]

Fortunately, it is not necessary to reinvent the wheel when a new church is started. Those who wish to start a church can identify and replicate what Nazarenes do well and do that with excellence. For example:

• **Nazarene pastors are upbeat and positive.** The *FACT* survey suggested a variety of descriptions of churches for respondents to choose from in describing their churches. The responses from Nazarenes imply local church leaders possess positive attitudes. Of course, not all pastors are upbeat, and probably no pastor is upbeat all of the time. But Nazarene pastors tend to be positive in their descriptions of the churches they serve. This same attitude shows in their preaching and their contacts with people.

• **Nazarene worship is generally uplifting.** Most Nazarene pastors (82 percent) say their worship services are spiritually uplifting and inspirational. Most of these congregational leaders also say the sermon in their worship service often or always focuses on personal spiritual growth (96 percent), personal commitment and/or conversion (94 percent), and God's love and care (91 percent).

• **Nazarenes value relationships within the church.** Most pastors say their congregation feels like a close-knit family (74 percent). Most believe their congregation's programs and activities strengthen personal relationships among participants (62 percent). And a majority say new people are easily incorporated into the life of the congregation (56 percent). In fact, close-knit families usually find it harder than other families to welcome new people into the group. This may explain the lower percentage agreeing with the description about incorporation. New churches may be more attractive because new people do not have to work their way into an already established, close-knit group.

• **Nazarenes seek spiritual vitality.** Nearly two-thirds (64 percent) of the pastors say their congregation is spiritually vital and alive. Nearly as many (63 percent) say their congregation helps members deepen their relationships with God.

• **Nazarenes value the past and are committed to the future.** A majority (60 percent) of Nazarene pastors say their congregation clearly expresses its Nazarene heritage. Sixty-four percent say their congregation is a moral beacon in the community. More than half (58 percent) say their congregation welcomes innovation and change. Two-thirds (66 percent) say their members are excited about the future of their congregation.

Now a Challenge to NewStart Pastors and Core Groups

Thousands would turn to Christ and become Nazarenes if they knew us at our best.

Here's the challenge. Don't hide our identity as you start a new church. Instead, give our strengths high visibility and live up to them with excellence and joy. Then your new people will have the best of historic Christianity plus the added emphasis on the biblical promise of a clean heart and a holy life—the best way of life ever offered to the human family.

Needed: Missional-Minded Women to Start New Churches
Giving Your Call to Ministry an Address and Zip Code
RICHARD HOUSEAL

LIKE UNCLE SAM'S "I NEED YOU!" SLOGAN from the war years, women are needed to start new churches in the Church of the Nazarene. This SOS plea for a wholehearted investment of one's life and ministry in starting new churches is not an entirely new challenge in Nazarene history. Rather, it is a call to replicate the incredibly effective part women played in starting new churches when the denomination was young.

Between 1920 and 1935, women made up 10 to 12 percent of the pastoral workforce and 20 percent of all ministry roles in the Church of the Nazarene.[1] According to Rebecca Laird, "An oft-repeated folklore tells us that Phineas Bresee, one of the main denominational founders, was fond of saying, 'Some of our best "men" are women!'"[2]

Without a doubt, now is the time for some of our best NewStart leaders to be women. Or should I say, now is the time for some of our best women to become NewStart pastors. Either way—women are needed for this ministry.

NewStart is a new opportunity for the church to empower women to fulfill their God-given call to ministry. At the same time, NewStart provides a contemporary spiritual pioneer opportunity for women of this generation to follow in the footsteps of Nazarene legends such as Emma Irick and Deona McCraw Smith. The essential issue is to fulfill the Great Commission more effectively than ever and at the same time provide ways for women to answer the call to ministry God has placed on their lives.

Even though the Church of the Nazarene has always ordained

women for ministry, there have been—and still are—barriers to women in ministry. C. S. Cowles, Rebecca Laird, Edward Lehman, and others have adequately written about these theological, cultural, and structural barriers, so I need not address them again. However, many of us believe those barriers need to change radically. And we seek to lower them in as many ways as possible. The time for analysis is past, and the time for action has arrived.

A Call to Move Beyond Debate to Action

NewStart offers one way to help correct the problem. NewStart offers opportunities that minimize barriers and maximize the use of your skills. Here's the challenge to every woman in ministry or those contemplating ministry—why not use NewStart to bypass many barriers and at the same time fulfill your ministry by leading new people to Christ?

What would 200 new churches started in the right way by women pastors do for lost people? And what would it do to tear down existing prejudices and barriers?

▷ ▷ ▷

Why not use NewStart to bypass many barriers and at the same time fulfill your ministry?

▷ ▷ ▷

Think of the possibilities—women with missional spirits becoming redemptive pioneers. It might happen through local churches adding a woman staff member with the stated intention that in a year's time she will lead a core group of laypeople to start a new church. Or it could happen by having women who already lead compassionate ministry centers use those ministries as a foundation for beginning a new church. Or it could occur through women starting Bible studies to form a nucleus for a vital new church.

When Paul sent Phoebe to the church in Rome, he "commended" her to them and told them "to receive her in the Lord in a way worthy of the saints and to give her any help she may need from you, for she has been a great help to many people, including me" (Rom. 16:2). Though the apostle may not have been specifically referring to starting new churches, NewStart does provide an effective way to "commend" women to Churches of the Nazarene everywhere as potential pastors for one of the most significant assignments the denomination has to offer—starting strong new churches the right way.

Door Opens with General Superintendents' Declaration

A wonderful new door opened potentially for women in 1997 when the general superintendents declared the United States and Canada to be mission fields. Women have always played key roles in Nazarene missions. Does it not follow logically that they should be key players in opening North America as a mission field?

The late Charles Morrow, Nazarene missionary to Haiti, used to say, "The Church of the Nazarene in Haiti was built on the backs of women." The same is true in many mission fields around the world where women have worked to start, maintain, and grow churches. The record of starting churches is strong and impressive.

Could it be that the renewed North American missional emphasis to start strong new churches offers women opportunities to fulfill their call to ministry? Could it be that those whom God has called to ministry of either gender but who have not been called to a specific assignment by a local congregation might become pioneers in an adventuresome, cutting-edge place of service in the NewStart revolution? Is NewStart an answer to the prayers of those who are frustrated because no local church has called them to an assignment? Is this God's nudge for women and for our denomination to claim the promise of Acts 2:17-18 (emphases added):

In the last days, God says,
   I will pour out my Spirit on all people.
Your sons and *daughters* will prophesy,
   your young men will see visions,
   your old men will dream dreams.
Even on my servants, both men *and women*,
   I will pour out my Spirit in those days,
   and they will prophesy.

Global Missions Has High Involvement of Women Leaders

Women's wholehearted involvement with global missions goes back to the early part of the 19th century with the formation of organizations such as Female Foreign Missionary Societies. By 1929, 67 percent of missionaries in six different Protestant denominations were female.[3]

In the Church of the Nazarene, women have given strong leadership to Nazarene Missions International since the beginning. In fact, one wag who was also a male pastor was overheard to say, "For a man to try to break into leadership in the district missionary council is about as hard as a woman trying to get a pastorate."

With the United States and Canada being recognized as a mission field and with the missional mind-set now sweeping across our denomination, this is a good time for women to step forward to take a major servant role in starting new churches.

Faithful Achievement Needed to Start Strong New Churches

Next the achievement question must be raised. Will women, just like some men, commit to all-out Kingdom efforts so something redemptive and holy and miraculous happens in the churches they start? Will they win new people? Will they build strong churches that win worldlings and provide strength for the saints? NewStart has little room for failure, so those starting churches must succeed. No question, women NewStart leaders can succeed, but none can excuse their failures because of gender.

Women NewStart leaders will likely do well just as the women leaders did in Korea.

Dr. Paul Y. Cho, pastor of the world's largest church, broke through the cultural barriers in his Korean society and placed women as leaders within the church. Cho writes, "God then showed me that we should use women as cell leaders. This was totally revolutionary to us, not only as conservative, Bible-believing Christians, but as Koreans."[4]

Cho goes on to advise,"In all of the years I have been teaching the cell system, I found that my female associates have been loyal and reliable. They have . . . worked hard. My advice to you then is, 'Don't be afraid of using women.'"[5] God has blessed Cho's willingness to use women in leadership positions, and the kingdom of God is greater for it.

MEET NEWSTART WOMEN PIONEERS

Let's get acquainted with gifted Nazarene women who have served or are now serving as church starters.

• **Meet Elsie Wallace.** I'm not sure Elsie Wallace intended to pastor a new church. Soon after she and her husband, DeLance, moved to Spokane, Washington, she was asked to serve as pastor of the newly organized rescue mission located on a city block that was "literally filled on its four sides with saloons and places of wickedness."[6]

In fact, five years later, in 1902, when the mission was organized as a church with 50 charter members, Elsie still didn't have a preacher's license, but she was unanimously called as the church's first pastor.

Spokane First Church grew out of that mission and during its 99th year—2000—received 106 members by profession of faith and reported an annual worship attendance of 753.

It was small steps of faith that brought Elsie Wallace to the task of pastoring a new church. She questioned her abilities in her first letter to Dr. Bresee: "I feel my utter helplessness and ignorance and our Lord must give wisdom, for this work is His, and we His Bride. Hallelujah! At your earliest convenience—we hope not later than in April—we want you to come up and 'straighten us out,' and in every way shepherd your 'youngest lambs.'"[7]

Rebecca Laird writes that "DeLance recognized that Elsie possessed better gifts and graces for pastoral ministry." And an article in *The Pentecostal Messenger* reported that Pastor Wallace "is indeed one of the best pastors we ha[ve] ever seen anywhere, and is doing a great work."[8] Mrs. Wallace was instrumental in starting other new churches in the Northwest and even served for a time as district superintendent of the Northwest District.

• **Meet Emma Nees.** In contrast to Elsie Wallace, Emma Nees knew she was called to preach and to start new churches. Emma was saved in 1910 through the influential ministry of the Laymen's Holiness Association. Her husband, Lawrence Nees, was not yet a Christian.

But as Emma prayed for her husband's salvation, God was using the experience to develop a heart for seeing souls saved. After a few months, Emma led Lawrence to the Lord and they joined the Church of the Nazarene, a new Holiness denomination.

Soon they became a wonderfully inspiring church-starting team. Emma and Lawrence worked side by side starting churches throughout Montana in such towns as Elmsdale, Sidney, Helena, and Kalispell. Those who knew the Neeses said Lawrence was an inspirational leader, but Emma was the better preacher.

As the Nees family moved from town to town starting new churches, they had little—if any—outside financial support. So Lawrence secured secular employment to support the family while Emma preached and held services. The plan was for him to become the official pastor after the church had enough financial strength to support their pastor economically. That did not often happen because they never stayed very long in any one place—Emma knew that her calling was to start new churches wherever possible.

One of the churches the Neeses started was in Kalispell, Montana, with the help of a farming family surnamed the Wagners. This church, started in 1935, soon got off to a good numeric start because the Wagners had 9 children. To this day, the Kalispell church continues as a strong Church of the Nazarene on the Rocky Mountain District.

Even with their constant moving, Emma and Lawrence raised 12 children of their own. They stayed long enough at the Kalispell church for the Wagners' daughter Doretta to fall in love with their son Guy. The results of their church-starting ministry continue to bless the denomination to this day. The farmer's daughter and the preacher's son married and went into pastoral ministry. Their first child, Tom, was born in the parsonage next door to the church while a revival service was in progress. That baby was Tom Nees, who now serves as director of Mission Strategy in the USA/Canada Mission/Evangelism Department.

Think of the influence that church-starting family—Emma and Lawrence Nees—has had on the denomination. Their grandson's revolutionary ministry has effectively called the Church of the Nazarene back to its nearly forgotten roots of compassion evangelism. Their impact also continues through Tom Nees's leadership in the new missional emphasis. And who can even imagine the effect of their son Guy Nees's ministry as influential pastor in Canada, college pastor at Olivet, superintendent of the Los Angeles District, and world missions director.

• **Meet Rosie Moore.** Sister Moore, as her people call her, is a modern-day pioneer pastor who has started an African-American church in St. Louis. At the age of 53, Rosie started a Bible study in her home that later became St. Louis New Hope Church. The year was 1982, and the Bible study was on Thursday nights. Soon people began to ask for a Sunday morning service.

Though the Moores lived in an area that prohibited large meetings in a home, Rosie's neighbors allowed them to use the driveway and backyard for parking on Sundays. As the group grew, they started tithing. Soon they were looking for a larger place to meet. In 1985, what started as a Bible study in Rosie's home was organized as a church with 38 members.

The foundation for Sister Moore's ministry is the Scripture's promise of a pure heart. Rosie Moore testifies, "A clean heart cleanses away the need to hate, and lots of our people hate. God has called me to teach and preach the doctrine of a pure heart because it makes such a difference."[9]

Pastor Moore was ordained in 1990 and continues to pastor the church, which reported 184 members in 2000.

• **Meet Karen Seers.** The NewStart in West Cobb, Georgia, founded by Karen Seers, was also started as a Bible study. From the onset, this group was formed with the intention of becoming a NewStart. Seers had been a longtime member of the Marietta church when God placed the town of West Cobb and their need for a new church on her heart. As she shared her calling, the Marietta congregation began to understand their ministry as a sponsoring congregation. In the beginning days, Pastor Seers reported monthly to the Marietta church board. She says, "Having a strong sponsoring church has provided us a great start, and we are grateful."[10]

• **Meet the Woman in the Mirror.** I believe that God is calling women to be "modern-day pioneer" pastors in order to create a revolution of new churches and new-church workers. I also believe their churches will become miracle-transforming forces for God in the lives of thousands of people.

Is God calling you as He called Emma Nees to be a modern-day pioneer pastor in the ministry of starting new churches?

Perhaps you have never thought of the possibilities, satisfactions, or relationships NewStart can provide. Maybe you never considered the advantages of starting a church as compared with being called to pastor an established church. For example, one advantage for a woman NewStart pastor would be that everyone who committed to the core group and everyone who attended the church would realize from the start that it was served by a woman pastor. Thus old prejudices and silly debates would be unnecessary, in fact out of place, in light of the accomplishments.

WOMEN POSSESS NEWSTART CAPABILITIES AND GIFTS

It should not surprise anyone that women can be effective NewStart pastors. They possess many of the qualities needed by the pastor of a new church. In his manual *How to Select Church Planters,* Bob Logan lists 13 qualities to look for in a new church leader.[11]

1. Visionizing capacity
2. Intrinsically motivated
3. Creates ownership of ministry
4. Relates to the unchurched
5. Spouse cooperation
6. Effectively builds relationships
7. Committed to church growth
8. Responsive to community
9. Utilizes giftedness of others

10. Flexible and adaptable
11. Builds group cohesiveness
12. Demonstrates resilience
13. Exercises faith

What About Unique Feminine Qualities?

Obviously, many women possess all of these qualities in Dr. Logan's list—sometimes in greater abundance than men. But what about unique qualities?

For example, Christian family specialist Larry Crabb says, "A godly woman is more interested in giving whatever she has to meet someone's needs, . . . [and] she tends to value giving something of herself to nourish relationships and deepen attachments."[12]

Or what about Dr. James Dobson's description of the biological differences of women? To him these differences "[result] in a greater appreciation for stability, security, and enduring human relationships. In other words, females are more *future*-oriented [italics his]."[13] These traits square with Logan's visionizing and resilience capabilities, both of which are necessary qualities for a NewStart pastor.

Leadership Styles

The leadership style that many women demonstrate is also favorable to starting a new church. Edward Lehman's research finds that "women were more likely than men to try to give the congregation power over its own affairs."[14] In harmony with Logan's list of qualities needed in a new-church pastor, creating ownership of ministry will often be a quality found in women because their leadership style is to empower the congregation. This style of pastoral leadership is also an excellent fit for much of our society, which emphasizes empowerment and team effort. This quality also supports our theological understanding of discipleship and the priesthood of all believers.

Mothers and Fathers to a Congregation

Although a large amount of research shows differences between men and women, there is also reputable research that indicates men and women in ministry are often closer in personality traits than to their respective gender. A 1984 study by Bonita Ekhardt and W. Mack Goldsmith "found that male and female seminary students were more alike than different in their motivational profiles."[15] Their research also discovered that "male seminary students were higher than general college males on nurturance, succorance . . . and lower on autonomy.

Similarly, the female seminary students outscored the general college females on affiliation, dominance, exhibition, understanding . . . while scoring lower on aggression and change."[16] Their conclusion that male and female personality profiles tend to converge for those in the ministry supports the idea that God has given both men and women the necessary gifts and graces needed to start new churches.

Such needs for nurturing, caring leaders are connected in Pastor David Fisher's delightful book *The 21st Century Pastor*. He does this in a chapter titled "Both Mother and Father: The Pastor's Heart," where he calls attention to the apostle Paul's double metaphor for an effective pastor—a loving mother who cares for her children and a gentle father who encourages, comforts, and urges his family flock to live lives worthy of God.

Two quotes from Fisher may help deepen our understanding of the need for increased tenderness:

1. About a mother's tenderness in the pastor: "Few portraits of a mother are more mysteriously powerful than a mother nursing her child. . . . A mother always has a listening ear, a warm embrace, and an affirming word. Her acceptance has no limits, and her forgiveness no boundaries. She cannot give up on her own. Her heart has no eraser that can eliminate her love."[17] He continues to develop the motherly tenderness theme for the Christian pastor across several pages of his book.

2. About a father's spirit of encouragement in the pastor: "We assist the Great Encourager. . . . We are God's cheerleaders for His children. We ache for their success, and when their lives take on the character of the gospel, we have no greater joy."[18]

▷ ▷ ▷

It is obvious that women are capable of starting churches.

▷ ▷ ▷

Whether women or men generally possess stronger innate qualities for starting churches is a debatable and, for some, even an explosive question. I am personally convinced most women are more nurturing than men—a much-needed trait for new-church leaders. After all the debates are finished, whatever conclusion one reaches, it is obvious that women are capable of starting churches. And since they are capable, they must do it, and our churches must step forward to help as sponsors.

Getting a Clear Focus

As we have seen over and over, women can be effective church starters. The challenge to women called of God has never been greater because the need for new-church evangelism has never been greater. Whoever starts a church, whether a woman or a man, the focus of the strong new congregation must be the two interrelated components of the Great Commission—winning converts and discipling them in the faith. Writing in the *Nazarene Messenger* in 1903, Phineas Bresee said, "The time has come when it should be asked, in reference to any people or sect, large or small, do they do God's work in getting sinners converted and believers sanctified?"[19]

Why Not Start Now?

God be praised for women who have already started a church. But at the present time, these situations are too few to significantly impact the world. The denomination needs thousands more to become proactive—to become truly missional in an all-out commitment to new-church evangelism. Women are needed in that workforce to creatively exercise faith and start hundreds of churches.

There may be many women who have the gifts and graces necessary for starting a new church—and who may already have a significant ministry—but have not seen themselves as a pastor. Others may have sensed God calling them to pastoral ministry but have been unable to scale the barriers that society has placed before them. Still others may not be sure of their calling or how to get started on the journey. While there are probably hundreds of ways to start a church, here are a few ideas to get started.

1. **Start a Bible study with the intent that it will become a New-Start church.** Even in a church that does not have the dream of sponsoring a new church, nobody will be against starting a Bible study. A new Bible study group will be enthusiastically supported. Unchurched friends and relatives who currently are not interested in "church" could be the beginning target group. Other potential target groups could be new families moving into the area, immigrants that could use a Bible study to learn English, or single parents whose family life would benefit from a Bible study with their children and the support of others in their situation.

2. **Start a compassionate ministry center with the intent that it will become a NewStart.** Scripture tells us repeatedly to have compassion for the poor. Our response should include bringing them into the fellowship of the church. A compassionate ministry center creates new avenues into the lives of people who often do not have a church home. Nazarene Compassionate Ministries, USA/Canada, has a host of resources to help you start a compassionate ministry center. Start by browsing their web site at <www.nazarenecompassion.org>.

3. **Find a sponsoring church that will bring you on staff and allow you to mine a NewStart core group.** This technique is already being used by a number of sponsoring churches. Women are often hired for associate staff positions. In fact, 33 percent of ordained or district licensed women are in staff positions at local churches. No other role in the church has more women, including the number of women who are currently unassigned. Those currently serving in a staff position could ask their pastor to pray about becoming a new-church sponsor. The church would become a sponsor by allowing its associate to gather a core group of people for a NewStart. For those whom God has called to pastoral ministry but are having difficulty receiving a call from a local church, pursue the idea of an associate position at a sponsoring church. The staff experience and sponsoring church will provide preparation for anyone's ministry.

SEEK THE FATHER'S DIRECTION

The Church of the Nazarene needs called women of God to start new churches as His ministry assignment for them. When writing about women in the early years of the Church of the Nazarene, Rebecca Laird states, "Most served as pastors or leaders of organizations they had founded. They did not passively wait for a congregation to recognize their gifts."[20] Perhaps some closed door may be God's signal—start a church.

Perhaps some closed door may be God's signal—start a church.

Undoubtedly there are Nazarene women involved in outreach programs and compassionate ministries who have never seen themselves as "preachers or pastors." Or maybe some have sensed God's call to ministry but have not been able to reconcile the call with their family's commitments. According to Laird and her research, these women are not alone. She writes, "A . . . theme that appears in the lives of at least half of these early women preachers is the struggle to accept the call to preach. Such a call was often thought inappropriate and out of line with the expectations of family, society, and church." She goes on to say, "None of these women blithely decided one day to preach. An inner transformation had to take place."[21] Our prayer is that God will use this book to continue that inner quest for direction. We firmly believe that God is calling women into His service as pastors and that NewStart is a tool to accomplish His purposes.

Mission Strategy in the USA/Canada Mission/Evangelism Department provides many valuable resources including the following:

• Training materials, seminars, and programs to promote female leadership

• Support and direction for language and racial minority strategy committees planning for evangelism and church growth through female leaders

• Scholarships to full-time minority female students preparing for the ordained ministry

• A referral service of female pastoral candidates to district superintendents

ARE YOU READY TO TAKE THE FIRST STEP?

Here is an adaptation of a powerful phrase from Roger Babson, founder of Babson-United, Inc.: "The successful [woman] is the one who had the chance and took it."[22] Though Babson never heard of NewStart, his words might become the catalyst to push you to do something great for God and lost people. NewStart may be that opportunity. Take it.

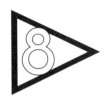

How to Start Churches for Cultural and Minority Groups

Turning Mission at Our Doorsteps into Vibrant Churches

OLIVER R. PHILLIPS

HISTORIANS AND SCHOLARS ALIKE cite the period between 1860 and 1930 as years of the most unprecedented church membership growth in American history. And the apparent reasons for this expansion coincided with an upsurge in religious diversity, cultural diversity, European immigration, and a degree of religious tolerance. Since history tends to repeat itself, our present-day immigration and diversity may provide similar opportunities for the church in our time. But to see the opportunities requires that we know what is happening and that the church respond with understanding, sensitivity, and something worth coming for.

THE CHANGING FACE OF USA/CANADA

Today, America stands in the middle of a multicultural revolution. No longer are the United States and Canada countries where differences in race and culture can be ignored or even deaccentuated. Every village, community, school, town, institution, and place of employment bring us face-to-face with the reality that these countries have become a salad bowl of minority groups, languages, and cultures.

God has brought the world's mission field to the front door of every American and Canadian. Look back over any day and try to remember how many people you've observed of color and/or with some strange language accent. Although most new Americans used to settle in East or West Coast areas, they are now moving to smaller cities and towns in the heartlands where jobs have been offered.

Think of the possibilities for the church. One of its greatest opportunities in the new millennium lies in its ability to harness the assets of our cultural and racial diversity. For the Church of the Nazarene to remain true to the Great Commission, it must reach out to the nation's historic minorities and to the millions of immigrants who have made America home.

The changing face of America in the 21st century is composed of significantly different factors from the period 1860 to 1930. Immigration in the last 30 years has not been just European but Asian and Latin American as well. Since the Immigrant Act of 1965, larger groups of Asians are immigrating to the United States. This modern immigration is much different in color and origin than the almost lily-white European immigration early in the last century.

At the same time, we must learn lessons and gain strategies by listening to Michael Barone's idea that most Americans have some experience in their background as immigrants—either themselves, their parents, or their grandparents. Barone contends that the current Black experience resembles the earlier Irish experience, Latinos the earlier Italian experience, and Asians the earlier Jewish experience.[1]

Any way you count the numbers, they are staggering. The most conservative predicators estimate that by the year 2050, the present English-speaking white majority will comprise only one of a sizable number of minority groups that will collectively constitute the population of the United States. The Church of the Nazarene needs an intentional strategy designed to ensure its ability to capitalize on the opportunities God is providing. To do less would be poor stewardship.

Consider the following statistics to support these observations:

• More Jews live in America than in Israel.

• More persons of African descent live in America than any country except Nigeria.

• More Samoans live in America than in Samoa.

• More Hispanics live in America than any country except Mexico or Spain.

• More Hispanics will live in America than the total population of Canada.

• More Cubans live in Miami than any other place, except for Havana.

• More Armenians live in Los Angeles than any city in the world.

• And the growth continues—in the United States in the '90s, the Asian population grew by 107 percent, Hispanics by 53 percent, Native Americans by 38 percent, while the general population grew by 6 percent.

These incredibly amazing realities should awaken us to the challenge of becoming the New Testament church in this new century. Dr. Bill Sullivan, director of USA/Canada Mission/Evangelism, succinctly warns, "The Church of the Nazarene will rise to the challenge, or it will falter, flounder, fail, and fade." Of course, the church cannot go back to tunics, oxcarts, snail-paced living, an agricultural society, insidious poverty, unheated sanctuaries, and hour-long sermons. What we need is the spirit of the pioneers—their sacrifice, their do-or-die commitments, their mission-focused efforts, and their all-out connection with Jesus—to be taken to our new neighbors. The goal is to win them to the Lord, disciple them so they become Christ-centered disciples, and make a transforming change in our present-day society.

Though this challenge of unbelievable proportions may surprise us, it happened before the beginning of the 21st century. Dr. Cheryl Sanders, professor of church ethics at Howard University School of Divinity and pastor of the historic Third Street Church of God in Washington, D.C., stated at the Multicultural Ministries Conference held at Bethany, Oklahoma, 1998, "So how is it that the church is just now becoming multicultural, if the Bible says it was born multicultural? Because of Pentecost, we should divest ourselves of the idea that an inclusive, multicultural church is something new, or something we should pride ourselves for thinking up at the close of the twentieth century."[2]

THE PRESENT OPPORTUNITY AND OBLIGATION

It is possible that the church of the 21st century will more closely resemble the Pentecostal crowd of Acts 2, where worshipers came from the present-day lands of Iran, Iraq, Israel, Lebanon, Cyprus, Malta, Syria, Jordan, Egypt, Libya, Saudi Arabia, Turkey, Greece, Albania, Italy, and parts of Asia. The present immigration phenomena are indeed rapidly moving the United States from merely a repository for European offshoots to a multicultural world nation with cultural ties to virtually every race and area in the world. By divine providence the stage has been set for a 21st-century church growth revival. The field is indeed ripened unto harvest.

To be a truly missional church means to be in touch with the need to reach out to the new neighbors who merge into our communities. The Great Commission remains the rallying cry for the church, but the doing of ministry does not take place in a vacuum. The relevant question for the church today is how to implement effective evangelism in the midst of this flourishing pluralism in society and community. How does a predominantly white denomination become missionally evangelistic within a changing multicultural nation?

If the influence of the congregation is to establish new frontiers, respect must be shown for the rituals and reality that bespeak other peoples' deep belief in the history that made their existence possible.

It is with forceful perception that Dr. Tom Nees, director of Mission Strategy for the Church of the Nazarene, observes the church's dilemma. He states, "I fear that if we continue to do nothing different than we are doing, in the near future, when and where there is no majority group, this denomination will be marginalized as a predominantly English-speaking white fellowship in a sea of diversity."[3] It can no longer be business as usual. Nees warns that our objective should not simply be to start culturally specific churches. This initiative should be part of a more comprehensive strategy to make all churches display the welcome mat for all peoples.

That challenge creates a dilemma for both the predominant white church as well as culturally specific churches. Let me explain. We need to start culturally specific churches that cater to the needs of people who find themselves comfortable in a particular cultural setting. A basic sociological principle proffers that people prefer to be with people like themselves. It is within this context of religious groups that a healthy social fabric is most naturally nourished, thereby establishing social solidarity. Churches exist to provide meaning, belonging, and security.

Now for the other side of the dilemma—according to the *1998 National Congregations Study*, about 90 percent of American congregations are made up of at least 90 percent of people of the same race.[4] Despite the seeming displeasure with this stark reality, we need to be careful not to attribute this congregational homogeneity to prejudice alone. If groups maintain their strength by providing meaning and belonging, the particularizing force of similarity must be acknowledged.

God works in the language and culture of those to whom salvation is offered. It is not necessary to surrender one's cultural identity in order to be a Christian. God uses one's ancestral identity as a legitimate gift, as well as a means of revealing love, peace, and justice to the world. Churches that reflect culturally distinct ministries are being used by God to reach unchurched people. These churches must never exclude people of other cultures, but because of their context and/or their calling, they are oriented to particular cultural, language, or geographical settings. As our surroundings become increasingly multicultural, especially in the urban communities, it is right that the people of those communities be given the opportunity of affiliating with a congregation that reflects their cultural heritage and meets their particular needs.

There are other factors that make it imperative to minister to a particular group of people. While some may suggest that we should minister to all people, it is also obvious that targeting a specific group may be the most practical thing to do. "God is no respecter of persons" (Acts 10:34, KJV). God loves all and "wants all men to be saved and to come to a knowledge of the truth" (1 Tim. 2:4). These scriptural idioms do not militate against selectivity in effective ministry. It is inconceivable to reach all people simultaneously with the gospel—as churches go, "one size doesn't fit all."

People like to worship with others who share similar cultural mores. If the neighborhood around a congregation has changed, and the congregation has not been able to minister to the new residents of different race and culture, it may want to consider starting a culturally specific or multicultural new church.

Any strategy to facilitate a multicultural denomination should fundamentally employ a four-pronged comprehensive approach:

1. Start churches that reflect the cultural composition of the community.
2. Start churches that cater to the myriad immigrant groups that are becoming a vital part of communities.
3. Start churches that are intentionally multicultural to provide a place of worship in multicultural communities.
4. Provide assistance to white as well as minority congregations who share a genuine commitment to racial and cultural diversity.

Starting a new church among another cultural group should be approached with a well-thought-out strategy. Fundamentally, starting a church in unfamiliar settings is similar to entering someone else's home without permission. How do we gain entrance into foreign territory and at the same time create a favorable structure for receptivity? In the midst of the cultural and religious pluralism of our new communities, we are called to present our faith without alienating or patronizing the people we intend to reach.

The New Testament Church probably faced similar seemingly insurmountable odds. Paul the missionary had few advantages over us. The tools of analysis and research we use today were obviously not available to Paul. Nevertheless, Paul leveled the playing field by recognizing the enabling power of the Holy Spirit as central to his missionary pursuits. It is the Holy Spirit who taught the early Christians (John 15:26), guided them in the truth (16:13), filled them with strength (Acts 2:4), confirmed the preaching of the gospel with signs and miracles and empowered them to be witnesses of Christ (1:8). They were guided in their missional strategy (15:28), delegated others to share the responsibility of leadership (6:3), and increased the effectiveness of prayer (Rom. 8:26). This same strategy should be appropriated for starting churches in a different culture.

Regardless of the complex nature of starting new churches in a different culture, dependence on God and an acknowledgment of God's ultimate sovereignty over our efforts should be critically managed.

It is chiefly in the light of the changed demographic landscape that we are therefore called to engage in starting new churches. While we would be misguided in thinking that we can start new churches as clones of the sponsoring congregation, it is also true that we must seek to establish the basic elements of our heritage that are nonnegotiable. Our holiness core values must remain central to who we are. As a community of faith committed to clear denominational distinctives, we should be collectively permeated with the creedal, liturgical, and historical objectives.

GUIDELINES FOR STARTING CULTURAL AND MINORITY CHURCHES

What, then, are the guidelines that can ensure the starting of strong new churches in a different cultural surrounding? How can we deal effectively with the initial resistance to the replacement of established patterns of understanding who God is and what God does?

In any new venture for God, I like to visualize the whole process before I begin. Dr. David J. Hesselgrave, in his wonderful book *Planting Churches Cross-Culturally*, offers this seven-step way of developing such an overview:

1. Understand the task.
2. Analyze the task in the light of research and experience.
3. Identify helpful and useless approaches.
4. Make an overall plan to accomplish the task.
5. Gather the available resources.
6. Execute the plan.
7. Learn from experience, and use experience to fine-tune the plan.[5]

Preparing the Sponsoring Congregation

While there might not be universal agreement on the need to sponsor a new congregation, it is commendable to seek out individuals who share the same level of enthusiasm. Church expansion should never be a solitary exercise. The decision to start a new church is more than a routine process—it is an affirmation of the missional commitments shared by the community of Christians.

The pervasive consciousness of most members of the congregation makes it difficult for them to comprehend and respond to a call to starting a new church. Because most would like to see their church grow to a phenomenal size, starting a new church is often viewed as a step in the wrong direction. Throughout the close of the last millennium, the megachurch syndrome seriously shaped our perception of evangelism. However, there is a resurgence of new-church evangelism in many megachurches today. This apparent contradiction is not too dissimilar from churches of every size—shall we grow a big church or start a new church? In reality, one feeds the other.

Carl S. Dudley, an expert in ministry leadership development, suggests in his book *Basic Steps Toward Community Ministry* some appropriate steps that could be employed here to mobilize support for the intended ministry. Care should be taken to identify the congregation's assumptions, proclamations, and decision-making process. By so doing, one is made aware of the traditions and history of the congregation. Most congregations have their ministry anchored in themes of the gospel message.[6] For example, some groups hear God calling them to care for creation by emphasizing environmental awareness. Others hinge their ministry on responsibility and obedience to God by recognizing that there are ministries within the church that are responses to a particular expressed mandate. Once the historical tradition is recognized, the initiative to start a new congregation could be more easily presented as a responsive action. In his book *One New People*, Manuel Ortiz, professor of ministry and mission at Westminster Seminary, states, "Going back to tradition may serve the church well. Tradition can provide affirmation to a church that wants to make major transitions."[7]

A focus group could be formed to study the implications of the proposed ministry context. Who are the people in the congregation who can share in the passion? There may be individuals appropriately situated who, by virtue of previous relationships with other cultures, are an asset to the strategy. Identify persons in the congregation who have unexpressed links to the new culture. Seek out those who may want to participate on a support team to conduct community research.

The group thus convened can become a working committee designed to resource the effort or to be actively involved in the chosen task.

Build Bridges to Target Group

The mistake made so often with new-church starters is to attempt "bonding" without "bridging." Care must be taken to identify the factors that make the group a viable entity in the community. These are the threads that keep the pieces of the quilt together. A thorough understanding of the cultural models and the essence of the culture should be an imperative. Only by so doing could a healthy respect for a people be firmly established. The cliché most often used in faith-based organizations is, "The gospel must be edible to be credible." A bridge must be built with the new community.

There is no better way to build bridges with the new group than by paying attention to the felt needs, expressed or unexpressed. This can be accomplished by observing the populations and lifestyles, appreciating the historical changes and current trends, and by listening to the community. The sponsoring congregation should never assume that it understands what makes the other group tick or, for that matter, what makes it cry.

The new church started in a different community or among a particular group would not be an insulated organization. If it is to be a vital force in the community, it must cater to the whole human experience. It would be no use to pretend that physical and temporal needs are not integral to their receptivity of the gospel message. Bridges could be constructed with the institutions that give meaning to their lives. Getting to know the stakeholders in the community—such as teachers, taxi drivers, barbers, grocers, and other business owners—can be an invaluable asset.

Nehemiah magnificently exhibits this bridge-building process when he discovered the walls of Jerusalem in abysmal disrepair: "Then I said to [the Jewish people, the priests, the authorities, and the officials], 'You see the trouble we are in: Jerusalem lies in ruins, and its gates have been burned with fire. Come, let us rebuild the wall of Jerusalem, and we will no longer be in disgrace.' I also told them about the gracious hand of my God upon me and what the king had said to me. They replied, 'Let us start rebuilding'" (Neh. 2:17-18).

Study the Group and Its Culture

Form and practice from one culture may have a negative effect or impact on another culture. In order to reach any group with the gospel, we must love them as well as respect their cultural heritage. People are turned away from the gospel today, not by Christ, but by well-meaning zealots who bring their cultural baggage as an inseparable component of their faith. These individuals, while piously guarding their own culture, nevertheless expect others to commit cultural suicide by abandoning and divorcing themselves from their own people.

The Black church tradition is a case in point. One has only to sit through a service in an African-American church. There is a rich mixture of culture, religion, history, experience, African folklore, and eschatological hope. If a church is to be started in such a community, it cannot be a white church transferred to a Black community, nor can it be a white church that merely gives lip service to Black people. It must and should be a church that is shaped by the hopes and expectations of those who would cry, "Stony the road we trod!" William Smalley, in his explication of missionary anthropology, was right: "Even the most kindly intentioned among us takes it for granted that as our relationship with other ethnic people develops, it will do so on our terms. That is, we naturally expect these other folk will become like us, not that we shall become like them."[8]

But it doesn't work that way. If we are to start a new congregation that is truly indigenous of the people, respect must be given to their own culture.

Empower the Congregation

Unsuspectingly, we sometimes start churches that grow more and more dependent on the mother congregation rather than increase in independence. Nothing can contribute to the lack of growth and creativity within a new congregation as a structure that fosters prolonged dependence on the sponsoring congregation. It is true those minority groups and historic ethnic American groups may not possess the socioeconomic wherewithal to move toward financial independence as would other groups. This, however, should not be used as an excuse for continued dependence on the sponsor.

The multiplication church growth concept can only become viable as new congregations move toward independence. The relationship between the two congregations should be provisional and flexible, always anticipatory of something more, something greater. Partnership with the NewStart usually deteriorates if the subsidy mentality is allowed to impede nourished independence and individuality.

The sponsoring church must let the NewStart grow to responsible maturity. It will help and direct the daughter church at the beginning, but with maturity, "daughters" become mothers! From its inception, the new church must be taught that in time, it will also be expected to give birth to a new work. It is expected that the new congregation would become

1. self-sustaining financially,
2. self-governing as a local congregation,
3. self-propagating in its evangelistic programs.

With this vision, the congregation should desire to come to maturity, train leaders, begin new works, and extend God's kingdom by reproducing itself.

Leadership Development Among Minorities

In order for these new congregations to maintain growth and relevance, it will require leaders to be public theologians. As "ambassadors" for Christ (2 Cor. 5:20), they must stand between worlds, representing the distinctive vision and virtues of their particular cultural community of faith. This is sometimes difficult for the church starter of a different culture. However, the cross-cultural evangelist must move into the public arena with a profound sense of humility and reverence for the sacredness of people and their traditions.

Indigenous leadership should be encouraged. The leader of culturally specific congregations would do well to be grounded in and sensitive to the holistic ministry opportunities presented by the unique expression of community. Dr. Robert M. Franklin, president of Interdenominational Theological Center in Atlanta, Georgia, spoke to the issue of leadership in minority communities. Here are some desired descriptions for the leader of these new congregations, paraphrased from Franklin's observations:

• The leader should serve as an *anointed spiritual guide.* The leader understands his or her role in helping to transform present circumstances into holy encounters.

• The leader should be a *grassroots intellectual* who initiates and encourages informed public discussion on topics that matter most in people's everyday life.

• The leader should be a *civic enabler* who understands how to empower neighborhoods through both the political system, volunteerism, and advocacy.

• The leader should be a *steward of community economic development,* recognizing the potential economic power in aggregate income of the group.

• The leader should be a *cultural celebrant* who could design rituals to teach how traditional values could be brought into conformity with Christian beliefs.

> • The leader should be a *family facilitator*, designing programs to address the needs of single people, married couples, single parents, and others.

> • The leader should be a *technologically literate visionary*, aware of emerging technologies and trying to harness their potential to improve lives.[9]

Denominational Initiatives and Commitment

As a denomination, there can be a concerted effort to provide minority groups with the training that would be necessary to supply contextual leadership for the future. Minority and culturally specific membership growth will require an increased number of pastors with minority and culturally specific backgrounds and other professional leaders for the church, including leaders trained and developed at national and district levels.

There is an urgent need for contextual theological training for seminarians, pastors, and lay leaders having minority and culturally specific backgrounds, as well as leadership training for ministries focused on cultural contexts and on the church as a community-centered institution. Continuing education programs for pastors and professional development programs for staff positions in the denomination should be offered by seminaries. Our educational institutions and district training centers should be urged to have full-time minority faculty positions that are well informed and responsive to the needs of the various minority constituencies.

Our schools should also be encouraged to have minority visiting professors, mainly in the field of practical and ministerial theology, who are knowledgeable of and responsive to the needs of minority constituencies in the Church of the Nazarene. Adequate theological training must be provided for minority seminarians and pastors in pastoral ministry, Bible study, and evangelism. There should be aggressive intentionality with respect to minority representation on strategies to recruit and train minority leadership.

I'M GLAD THE CHURCH CAME TO THE WASHINGTON GHETTO

Twenty-six years ago, a small committed group of white Nazarenes started a church in the nation's capital in the midst of a poverty-stricken African-American neighborhood. The ministry focused on what was then considered to be a radical departure from the traditional forms of ministry. This community was still recovering from the civil unrest of the '60s. Everywhere one could see the results of inaccessible health care, high unemployment, homelessness, drug and alcohol abuse, dysfunctional families, and the latent incapacity to deal with systemic alienation and marginalization. Various structured ministries were started to address these problems. Ministry was to the whole person.

The worshiping corps on Sunday mornings comprised a healthy balance of residents of the Black community and the white Nazarenes. My first contact with this group was in 1977 when, as a suffering drug-abuse victim, I was accepted into this fellowship through their love and caring. I remember well the makeshift choirs, quartets, and hope-filled soloists.

Although the group never considered themselves to be church starters, they had indeed begun something that would blossom into a viable expression of the kingdom of God. There was always an unexpressed desire to see the community embrace and claim the church as theirs. Every effort was made to integrate African-American forms of worship into the service.

In April 1994, the local church board called me to be the second pastor in the church's history. At that time, the membership was 35 to 40 percent white. Over the six years that I was blessed to lead that congregation, I witnessed a significant change in the style of worship and other forms of praise and liturgy. Today, that congregation is 99 percent Black with a dominant African-American genre of worship.

The attraction to the neighborhood has come about through a gradual acceptance that the church is a haven in which people could find meaning, security, hope, friendship, and religio-cultural identity. To worship in that congregation is to encounter Black gospel music, rhythmic praise, vocal affirmations, unorthodox expressions of thanksgiving, spirited testimonies, and a total disregard for time. This is a significant transition. People from other cultures are not excluded from the worship experience, but there is a clear understanding that this is indeed a congregation where the preferred style of worship is Black.

By the way, the pastor who founded that congregation was Dr. Tom Nees. Serving now as the director of Mission Strategy at Nazarene Headquarters, Nees still resides in the Washington, D.C., area, and his membership is with this congregation, known as the Community of Hope Church of the Nazarene.

How Laypersons Can Start Churches

Laity Have Unique Contacts for Starting Churches

Bryon McLaughlin

LONGTIME NAZARENE FRANK DEAN was a boilermaker who traveled throughout the eastern United States building power plants and starting churches. If a job assignment kept him in any one place any length of time, he would put up a tent and hold services until there were enough converts to form a congregation. Quoting Vance Havner, Frank loved to say, "It's the preacher's job to fill the pulpit. It's our job to fill the pews."[1] He believed a church should be started wherever he discovered spiritual need.

Though pastors and district leaders have led the way in starting new congregations throughout much of Nazarene history, this task has never been limited to professional clergy alone. Pioneer Nazarenes believed that the message of full salvation was so important that they felt led by the Holy Spirit to share the message by starting churches everywhere. In response to that belief, many laypersons started churches in the early days.

A NEW IDEA THAT HAS WORKED FOR A LONG TIME

Lay involvement in starting churches is an idea as old as Christianity. The mandate for lay participation is implied, even if not explicitly stated, by Paul in Eph. 4:11-12: "It was he who gave some to be apostles, some to be prophets, some to be evangelists, and some to be pastors and teachers, to prepare God's people for works of service, so that the body of Christ may be built up."

In the Book of Acts, people with varying backgrounds and qualifications were effective church starters. Their drive for this work came from their own Upper Room experience with the Lord, which Lloyd John Ogilvie, Presbyterian chaplain of the Senate, described like this: "When He [the Holy Spirit] enters a human being, the mind is trans-

formed, the computer of the brain is given new data, the will is released from bondage, and the nervous system becomes the channel of
supernatural energy."[2] What a magnificent preparation for Kingdom
service, especially new-church evangelism.

After what happened in them in the Upper Room, their main pre-
requisite for starting a new church was a conviction that God had
"sent" them to a place to bear witness to Jesus. They soon discovered
that whenever anyone believed their witness, a fellowship of believers
was needed to strengthen, instruct, and encourage the new converts.
Then, as now, churches were needed to conserve the fruits of evangelism efforts.

As they started congregations for discipling the new believers,
they discovered a wonderful serendipity of new-church evangelism—
new churches conserve converts, but they also attract new people who
do not know the Lord.

Though space limitation in this book prevents a full discussion of
the historical relationship between clergy and laity, Christianity started
as a lay movement. Jesus planted Christianity into the culture of His
time through people who were laity—that is, persons who earned their
living from sources other than the church.

E. Stanley Jones, the Methodist missionary-evangelist of a previous generation, may have overstated the case a bit but not much when
he wrote, "Jesus was a layman. . . . the apostles were laymen." Harnack,
the church historian, says that "all the early conquests of Christianity
were carried out by informal missionaries. Everyone who received the
gospel gave the gospel."[3] Read those staccato ideas again, and let them
sink in—those who received the gospel gave the gospel.

Jones continues with a discussion concerning credentials for doing ministry. He cites Jesus' reply to the question, "By what authority
do you do these things?" Remember His masterful reply: "The blind
see, the lame walk, lepers are cleansed, the deaf hear, the dead are
raised. The wretched of the earth learn that God is on their side" (Matt.
11:5, TM).

Neither the New Testament nor the Early Church distinguishes between laity and clergy as we do today. Some scholars say the first distinction between the two occurs in writings from 1 Clement in about
A.D. 95. "Laity" is from the Greek word *laos,* which means "common
people" as opposed to "professionals" or "royalty." Drawing from the
idea of God's covenant relationship to Israel, the New Testament often
uses *laos* to refer to the Church as the people of God.

Eventually, however, as the Early Church continued to expand, "professional clergy" were needed to preserve the work, so they were commissioned and given authority to do "full-time" ministry.

That development produced many benefits but also inhibited lay participation. Ministry roles became blurred, which prompted some laity to opt for spectator status and move from the sweat and passion of the playing field to the bench or the sidelines. But that was not the intent. Adding the professional clergy was planned to stimulate increased lay involvement through the training and equipping of the people of God for ministry. The Early Church grew because the ministry of the church was considered to be the normal expression and responsibility of all believers. They had found spiritual transformation, and the news was too good to keep.

John Wesley understood and used the powerful partnership of clergy and laity when he employed "lay" preachers to oversee small groups who gathered regularly for worship, prayer, instruction, and fellowship. These "lay" preachers often consulted with ordained clergy to decide what to teach and how to catechize new converts. The work of "lay" preachers contributed greatly to the evangelization of the hard-to-reach "working classes" and eventually played a part in social reform in Wesley's time.

Just as is true today, Wesley faced the mathematical factor of starting new groups. He realized that if new-church evangelism was left to the clergy to accomplish, there were simply not enough ministers to get the work done.

LAY INVOLVEMENT IN STARTING CHURCHES— PART OF A NEW REFORMATION

In recent days, church leaders are calling for a "New Reformation" among God's people for starting new churches. In the Protestant Reformation of the 16th century, emphasis was placed on the priesthood of all believers, justification by faith, and Scripture alone. Luther gave the Bible to all believers, and the church has never been the same since.

Today, the church is witnessing another reformation. New-church evangelism is being released to *all* believers—lay or ordained, male or female, young or old. This emphasis does not devalue the professional clergy but returns to the New Testament ideal that the role of laity is incredibly important—more than that, it is vital for the advancement of the kingdom of God in our time.

A key leader in the present-day missional movement, Charles Van

Engen, says laypersons too often fall into the "Santa's Helper Syndrome." That is, they come to believe their role for ministry is limited to the internal workings of the church rather than "ministry" in the world, which they perceive to be the role of the professional minister.[4]

Let's get the message clear. God, through the Holy Spirit, empowers all people, whether lay or clergy, to build His Church. In response, laypersons need to be alert to the Spirit by spending time with the Scriptures, listening in prayer, sharing ideas and concerns with others, and getting to know their community and community needs.

Lay participation in new-church evangelism should not be seen as a substitute for clergy involvement but as a whole additional workforce. Laypersons bring a unique set of skills, gifts, and connections that many pastors do not have. Laity are not better or stronger or weaker than pastors, just different. Due to their employment in the world, laity have a far greater opportunity to touch unsaved people with the gospel than do pastors.

God Empowers All to Build His Church

God's urgent mandate to His Church is to reach all people with the gospel. If that is to happen in sufficient numbers to impact our world, we must get the message out that the work of starting new churches is the privilege and responsibility of every believing Christian.

For laypersons who may feel overwhelmed by the possibilities of starting a new work, it is good to remember what one veteran lay church starter affirmed: "We don't start churches—God does!" That means we offer ourselves. We do everything we know to do and do it well. Then He does the rest.

In Acts 1:8, Jesus tells His Church, "But you will receive power when the Holy Spirit comes on you; and you will be my witnesses in Jerusalem, and in all Judea and Samaria, and to the ends of the earth." Notice, there is no "clergy only" sign on the assignment and promise.

A Nazarene businessman skilled in strategic planning is now applying his expertise to help start churches in Colorado. Wes Eby and Nancy Zumwalt, both former teachers skilled in English as a second language (ESL), have developed teaching materials Nazarene churches are using to start ESL classes. Such classes have led to the development of new multicultural congregations. Through denominationally sponsored ministries like Work and Witness (W&W) and Nazarenes in Volunteer Service (NIVS), many Nazarene laypersons are sharing their skills and training in building construction, agriculture, teaching, and medicine to build new churches in needy and remote areas of the world. Why not multiply that effort and commitment in the new mission field—the United States and Canada.

As Paul said in 1 Cor. 12:14, "Now the body is not made up of one part but of many." Being effective at starting new Nazarene congregations means creatively finding ways to reach out to the mission field around it.

▷ ▷ ▷

To commit to being a missional Christian means seeing ourselves as missionaries where we live and work.

▷ ▷ ▷

Often a layperson can start a Bible study or small group in a workplace or community where a pastor could never go. Charlie Wagner and Jerry O'Neal and their families had been driving 40 miles to attend a Church of the Nazarene. Feeling a need to start a church in their county—Calvert County, Maryland—they built a core group by using existing contacts and reaching out to community teens and their families. Groups of unchurched teens were taken to outings, Christian music concerts, and on retreats. As other families joined in, the core group met in a local elementary school for Bible study. Programs were developed for children and youth. Eventually, a congregation was formed, but only after Charlie and Jerry spent time developing relationships with persons in their community. They did what hundreds of Nazarene laypersons could do and do well if they seek the Lord's direction concerning a new work.

LAITY ARE NEEDED TO START CHURCHES

Nazarenes are using a new word—"missional"—to describe what has characterized an essential part of Christianity from the beginning, that is, extending the influence of Christ outside the church walls into the needy world around us. Thus, to commit to being a missional Christian means seeing ourselves as missionaries where we live and work. It means thinking of our churches as mission stations. It means seeing our communities as mission fields. And it means taking a significant part in the great effort of new-church evangelism so more people may learn about Christ.

For missional churches to emerge, all the people of God must be "equipped, enabled, organized, and inspired to participate in God's mission in the world." [5] That includes starting strong new churches in the right way in the right place.

This reformation that is now in progress calls for every lay Christian to become involved in some meaningful way in starting new churches.

As salt and light in the world, to use Jesus' metaphors, the people of God going about their work while they live as authentic Christians gives lay Christians enormous influence and hundreds of contacts in their world. Those contacts provide a ready-made seedbed for starting a new church.

Nearby Mission Fields

The reasons many laypersons have never started a church is that they have never been challenged by the opportunities or perhaps never felt they had permission from their pastors and other church leaders to do so. A whole new tide of permission and passion for starting new churches is sweeping across our denomination. The message is just do it in the name of the Lord, and He will go with you.

As people on the front lines, laity have a remarkable opportunity to make a difference in their own mission fields—their workplaces, neighborhoods, and communities. The opportunity to start strong new churches is limited only by creativity and imagination and the precise call of God to a given neighborhood. Or maybe church starting has only been thought of as something that was to be done far away and by someone else. Either way, the late General Superintendent V. H. Lewis explained nearby opportunities all people possess in these clear-as-day sentences: "The front line is always right next to you. The man who works next to you, the woman who sits at the next desk, the one who is sitting by you on the bus, train, or plane, the family living in the next apartment or next door. . . . the harvest field is right next to each of us."[6]

When laity are grasped by the gospel mandate to reach out to those around them, they become a force for growing existing churches as well as starting new ones.

Everyone Can Do Something

The big picture is not to start more churches or grow the denomination but to win more people for Christ. The Nazarene NewStart ministry is a well-designed program that has been field tested and approved by the denominational leadership that gives local churches—and the persons who attend those churches—permission to start new works.

The dream is for all laity to be involved someway in starting a church.

Like our church's global missionary efforts, everyone will not go, but everyone can give and pray and boost. Some can build buildings. Some can become missionaries on loan to a new work. Some can offer prayer, monetary support, or needed supplies to help start a new church. Some can become pioneers for starting new works. The Lord of the church will surprise some with a call to become leaders and church starters. Some will become members of core groups who are the key personnel in starting new churches.

Thinking Outside the Box

Risktakers are needed. People willing to think outside their comfort zone are especially needed. Or as one lay member of a core group said, "I am learning to think outside the box that I have been in all my life. It's frightening and fulfilling at the same time." While the challenge of starting new churches is great, the rewards are equally as great—and often greater.

▷ ▷ ▷

People willing to think outside their comfort zone are especially needed.

▷ ▷ ▷

When you think of people with whom to start making contacts, consider your unchurched neighbors and relatives. Consider international students, immigrants, and various minorities who have moved to almost every section of the United States and Canada. Missional opportunities abound in nearly every language and culture.

For example, several hundred Hispanic men were recruited to work in a meatpacking plant in a small town in the heartlands. Their families soon followed, and the little town that had never had any multicultural people was shocked and angry. They even said someone is stealing our town. But right in the middle of the confusion, the missionary council at the Church of the Nazarene went to work. They quieted fears. They told their neighbors these were people to whom their church had always sent missionaries. They helped the newcomers secure furniture and linens and medical care. Soon they organized a Hispanic church and shared their church facilities with the new congregation. Previously, the sponsoring church ran about 80 in worship; now the two congregations run close to 200 in total attendance.

Dr. Bill M. Sullivan, director of USA/Canada Mission/Evangelism Department, explains an essential quality needed to start new churches: "Some people can take something and make it bigger, but there are only a few that can take nothing and make something out of it—these are the people that can start churches." That capability may be polished and ready for use among many laypersons who think in such visionary ways at their jobs or at home.

Consider the story of Gilbert Dancey. Years ago, after a long and successful career as a Chrysler executive, Dancey retired to his boyhood home of Mount Jefferson, North Carolina, where there was no nearby Church of the Nazarene. Undaunted, he started a Bible study for neighbors, friends, and anyone who would come. The group grew, and the time came to start a church. However, there was no money or pastor available. Discouraged, he approached his district superintendent, Bill M. Sullivan, who suggested that Gilbert pastor the church until a minister could be called. Dancey objected but later agreed and accepted the challenge. For one year, he performed the role of pastor and continued to build the church. He did whatever was necessary. Sometimes that meant juggling finances or staying up late with a family in crisis. When doubts threatened the budding congregation, Dancey's leadership kept the church intact. When a pastor accepted the invitation to come, he found a strong congregation—but only because Gilbert made "something out of nothing."

HOW LAYPERSONS CAN START NEW CHURCHES

Listed below are some of the ways laypersons are starting new congregations in the Church of the Nazarene. The starting place for every individual is to ask the Lord to help you see ways you can become involved in starting new churches.

1. Do What Needs to Be Done

Marilyn Denson prayed 20 years for the unmet physical and spiritual needs of her students and their families at Greenvale Elementary School in urban Oklahoma City. After one of her students was tragically shot and killed, she knew something needed to be done. "Most of our children come from the projects. Sometimes buses come into our neighborhood and take children to church, but our children need to know that God is available for them in their neighborhood."

As a longtime member of Bethany First Church of the Nazarene, Marilyn shared her pain and brokenness with members of the pastoral staff. Her dreams for a church presence in the Greenville area prompted a unique collaboration between Bethany First Church, the districts of Northwest and Southwest Oklahoma, and Southern Nazarene University. The result was the birth of New Life Community Church.

The impact of New Life was virtually felt overnight. Today in that community, crime is down, relationships are being restored, and lives are being transformed by the gospel. By simply sharing the need and casting a vision, Marilyn Denson set in motion a blessed chain of events that started a church in a needed area.

Sometimes all that is necessary to start a church is to make others aware of an existing need.

2. Start a Small Group

Several years ago, a group of five retired Nazarene couples moved to the small mountain town of Buena Vista, Colorado. With no Church of the Nazarene nearby, they decided to form a Bible study group. As the group expanded, they rented a building to hold meetings. After a year, they worked with district church officials to form an official Church of the Nazarene. They called a pastor, and the church has steadily grown into a viable congregation—largely because of the vision and support of members of the Bible study group. Small groups like the one at Buena Vista are typical of how many new congregations get started.

The idea of small (or cell) groups is not a new phenomenon. Many variations exist to nurture believers or start new congregations. John Wesley, a theological forebear of the Church of the Nazarene, implemented the principle of small groups (called "classes") as a vehicle for church growth and renewal. By the end of the 18th century, Wesley had developed more than 10,000 class meetings.[7] Many have followed Wesley to use small groups to start new churches.

Why not consider starting a small group as an outreach tool to begin a new congregation? While every small group is different, healthy groups typically focus on the following components:

- Knowing God through worship and prayer
- Knowing one another through fellowship
- Reaching out to non-Christians
- Developing disciples and training new leaders

3. Organize a Mission Group

Several decades ago, a Washington, D.C., congregation pioneered developing small groups, called "mission groups" or "task groups." Group members focused on listening to God for specific nearby missional assignments, perhaps in their neighborhood or community. As a result, rather than embracing a self-absorbed spirituality, these groups maintained that a serious inner pilgrimage with God should focus on and energize an outer expression of service in the world. Their guidance for new expressions of Christian service came during prayer as they asked what God wanted done. One lay leader from that congregation explained, "The inward must not be sacrificed to the outward, nor the outward to the inward." Think of the hundreds of new churches that might be started if in hundreds of small groups every meeting closed with a prayer request: "Lord, show us what part You want us to have in new-church evangelism."

Imagine what would take place. New churches would spring up in hundreds of places. Laypersons would start a Bible study in their home that might eventually become a church. Some group members would be directed by God to become short-term NewStart missionaries. Some persons would be called to full-time service to start a new church. Others would give their time or abilities as laypersons to help start a new congregation. Listening and acting on God's missional directives has the potential of providing many adventuresome surprises for those who listen carefully to their Lord.

4. Reach Beyond Your Church—and Even Your City

For 20 years, Jane and Roger Howard happily attended Grove City, Ohio, Church of the Nazarene. Yet when Pastor Bobby Huffaker announced plans to launch a new congregation and asked church members to consider supporting a new church, the Howards felt led to go. Along with about 50 people, the Howards formed the core group of Hilliard Community Church. As part of a new congregation, the Howards labored on church committees to set up child care and a nursery, formed Sunday School classes and recruited teachers, and even helped develop a new church logo. The church began to attract new members, especially newly married couples and those with young families. Soon, many sought out Roger and Jane for advice on child rearing, finances, and other practical matters. As members in their 50s, they became "grandparents" of the young congregation. A retired schoolteacher, Roger's involvement led to a part-time position directing outreach. Jane complements Roger's work by planning social activities and working in the church's Hospitality Center.

Jane still works as a secretary at Grove City Church. She maintains that laity who help establish new churches don't have to completely cut ties with their former congregations: "We have maintained relationships with many of our friends from Grove City and sometimes attend special occasions. We realize we are in ministry together."

Sometimes NewStart evangelism reaches across long distances. In Olathe, Kansas, College Church is another example of laypersons leaving a home church to begin a new congregation—yet with a surprising new twist. Corey MacPherson, while serving as a seminary intern at College Church, was asked by New York District Superintendent Dallas Mucci to start a church in the Stony Brook area of Long Island, New York, after graduation. Corey shared his dream with Pastor J. K. Warrick. Warrick and others began to pray. After sharing Corey's plans with the church, Warrick called others to consider relocating to New York to establish a new congregation. The church gave $20,000 for relocation expenses. Although some people may relocate for a new job, 10 members of Olathe College Church moved across the country to establish a new church.

5. Creative Use of Work and Witness Teams

In 1991, the Cary Penny Road Church of the Nazarene on the North Carolina District faced extinction. For years, the struggling congregation met in a public school with no place to call home. High real estate and building costs made the prospects of a church building seem out of reach. Several members, weary of having no local church home, entertained thoughts of disbanding. A district Work and Witness team decided to help the local congregation build a 5,000-square-foot building on a handsome four-acre site on the edge of town. After 14 days a roof was built, and final construction was completed in a short time. Overnight, the congregation nearly doubled in attendance. Pastor Katherine S. Widdifield credits the district Work and Witness team with helping turn the church around.

In a similar fashion, laity can make a solid contribution to help new congregations develop facilities. Many laypersons have electrical, plumbing, and building expertise that can lead to the development of fledgling congregations. Under proper leadership, many youth groups could contribute significantly to help build churches. Consider using ministry or music teams of youth and even children to raise awareness and moneys toward the construction of a new church.

Ask God for New-Church Evangelism Eyes

The Scriptures are filled with examples of persons who recognized new realities and saw amazing possibilities for service and achievement after experiencing a life-changing encounter with God. Their own transformation prompted a desire to extend His kingdom into new frontiers in ways they had never previously considered. Sometimes they risked much to bring God's message to a needy world. That inner drive can become a passion for starting a new church near you.

Let's review the bedrock basics of new-church evangelism.

• God empowers all people to start churches.

• Laity are wanted and needed to start churches.

• Laity bring a unique set of skills, gifts, and relationships to new-church evangelism.

• Laity have connections in their workplace and community that enable them to become effective church starters.

• Laity can make other laypersons aware of a need for a new church.

• Laity can start small-group ministries that can become the catalyst for a new congregation.

• Laity can get involved in Work and Witness teams and in Nazarenes in Volunteer Service opportunities to start new churches.

Does God Want You to Start a Church?

Every believer has a God-inspired desire to fulfill Christ's mission in the world. As we have seen, research shows that the most effective outreach in our time is new-church evangelism. However, starting a church may sound so risky, so demanding, and so costly that you may be overwhelmed or frightened by the very notion.

Why not do what you can right now and see where it leads? The possibilities are endless. Start a mission focus group. Begin a Bible study in your home. Offer to develop a Work and Witness team for the newest church start on your district. Become a prayer partner with a church starter. Get involved in some aspect of new-church evangelism, and watch for your next assignment.

Jesus, the faithful Lord of the Church, will lead you in discovering your next step. Though you cannot do everything, you can do something. Ask God to direct your creativity and commitment to some worthy new-church evangelism cause.

NewStart's Search for Missional Entrepreneurs
Entrepreneurial Skills Discovered in Scripture
JIM DORSEY

RISK TAKING HAS ALWAYS BEEN a part of advancing the kingdom of Christ. Some say faith by its very nature contains the element of risk. Spiritual leaders throughout the Scriptures were risk-taking pioneers, from Moses and Joshua to Jesus and the apostle Paul. They stepped out into the unknown with confidence led by His Spirit. As one author wrote, "Paradigm pioneers have a different spirit than the naysayers about them. They have the ability to see a new thing, to perceive a bright future, to tap into the power of God."[1]

For first-century Christian leaders, ministry risks existed on multiple fronts. Imprisonment, financial ruin—even death—hovered over their endeavors from the political powers of Rome. Resistance and persecution from other established religious groups faced these missional pioneers in every city they entered. As strangers in foreign lands and hostile cultures, they endured the constant threat of undeserved and unexpected attacks. Usually when they entered a new area to begin their work, they experienced a revival or a riot, many times both. On top of those issues, the spiritual and emotional battles added even more difficulty. Not only did the powers of darkness resist their every effort for the Kingdom, but also the very people these missional pioneers tried to reach many times turned on them. Few are surprised to read of various members of these early pioneer teams just returning home in complete discouragement. For them the price seemed too high.

THE KEY STRATEGY

Yet even in intense hostile conditions, for others the vision remained crystal clear: spreading the gospel meant starting and growing new churches. However difficult the task, whatever the costs or personal risks, starting new congregations became strategic for leaders in the Early Church. For these pioneers, temporary risks were well worth the eternal gains.

Most of us remember the exciting story of the conversions in Acts 2, how the Lord added believers to the church daily. Their key strategy for missions found in Acts includes both the daily *addition* and *multiplication* of believers. These words from Acts 16:4-5 recently captured my attention: "Now while they were passing through the cities . . . So the churches were being strengthened in the faith, and were increasing in number daily" (NASB). Do you see it? Churches, as well as believers, were being added daily! You could assert new believers were multiplied daily *because* new churches were being added daily!

Most of our New Testament comes from various letters to these newly established fellowships of believers, a whole network of new churches in the making. As the number of churches increased, the number of new believers multiplied at an even greater proportion. And all this was accomplished when so much was on the line for them. This principle remains consistent today: the greatest method for winning people to Christ is starting new churches.

When you stop and think about it, they accomplished this incredible task with such limited resources. These missional entrepreneurs moved ahead in faith to new communities, sharing meager love offerings with those in need. They worked bivocationally to support their Kingdom-building activities. They had no financial backers. They owned no church buildings. When these spiritual pioneers ran into problems, all they could do was ask for God's intervention. And they did. And God intervened then as He still does now. Their Best Resource is ours too.

Genuine obedience to God's call to new-church evangelism does not wait for all the answers before responding. Somehow, someway, things had a way of working out in those early days of start-up missionary endeavors. Later they would testify that God supplied for "all [their] needs according to His riches in glory" (Phil. 4:19, NASB). At times, we need to be reminded again.

TWO GROWING MOVEMENTS

All around us, two silent movements have been spreading across the North American continent. Simultaneously across various denominations and congregations, a resurgence of starting churches is reaching new levels. Fuller Seminary reported in the late '80s and early '90s over 5,000 participants in their seminars on how to start new churches. Multiple denominations began creating their own departments for starting churches.

For the Church of the Nazarene, the all-out emphasis to start strong new churches the right way is called NewStart. This bold, new plan moves the permission, privilege, and responsibility for starting new churches to pastors and local congregations. All across the United States and Canada, hundreds of new churches are being started as a result of this movement, with existing Nazarene churches mothering new daughter congregations.

And the Church of the Nazarene is not alone with its priority for starting new churches. On one Sunday in 1987, one denomination launched 101 new churches on the same day—a record in missional endeavors! (Wonder who will break that record?) Without exception, research shows the growing denominations are those who are focusing on starting new churches.[2]

And about the same time, another development began capturing the attention of the American culture. Experts began predicting the "entrepreneurial movement" becoming more influential in this century than the industrial revolution was in the last. A Gallup poll revealed half of all adults today in the workplace want to own their own company. Most notably among graduating high school seniors, this entrepreneurial preference soars to 70 percent.[3]

Research also shows that the No. 1 reason many aspiring entrepreneurs never follow their dreams is the risk factor. What if their new businesses do not make it? How can they provide for their families if the new ventures are not successful? The uncontrollable variables that influence the success or failure of a new company create too much exposure for the faint of heart. The strategies for a new venture to tap into an existing customer base and win their loyalty appear too overwhelming. What if competitors in the area resist this new business coming to town?

In many ways, these issues reflect similar concerns for missional pioneers and NewStart pastors. Will the new church overcome resistance from both the existing churches and the post-Christian culture? How can NewStart pastors provide for their families while attempting to care for the needs of the growing family of God? Who will become the team of key players? Where do they worship? Missional entrepreneurs face an equal number of concerns in starting a new church—if not more. After all, their struggles also include the spiritual dimension.

THESE MOVEMENTS INFORM AND ENERGIZE EACH OTHER

You're probably wondering how these two movements come together. I'm glad you asked. Consider for a moment how these two trends are interrelated.

Entrepreneurs determine how to make the best possible use of the resources around them. They plan a careful course of action to lower the risks involved. They learn better ways to find the hard resources like facilities, money, gifts-in-kind, as well as the people with needed abilities to partner with them. At the same time, they learn how to better develop the unseen dynamic resources within people—the will to work, a sense of common goals, skills at vision casting, and how to encourage teamwork. And their checklist goes on and on.

Along with these two movements, the church is gaining a clearer understanding of its identity. As a Body of Christ, the church is not just another secular corporation. It has a unique mission in this world, and its leaders follow a divine call. But a special type of missional leader is needed for this task of starting new works. These Kingdom pioneers almost reflect an apostolic mind-set in their spiritual giftedness. The strengths of the missional entrepreneur help to discover, develop, and deploy all the hard and soft resources available to achieve the mission in starting new churches. Spiritual entrepreneurs have been the ones to lead the church into her greatest advances across the years. Many challenges now resemble those facing the Early Church. Consider just a few.

Existing religious groups continue to resist the arrival of a new church in their community, even now. The present culture attacks the basic tenets of the Christian faith. Financial pressures challenge at every turn. Emotional and spiritual pressures still weigh heavily on leadership. Many times, the unchurched target groups offer the greatest resistance to the whole endeavor in reaching them. But we know the temporary risks are still worth the eternal gains.

The United States and Canada have always been lands of opportunity for entrepreneurs—secular and spiritual. This common ambition evidenced today has never existed at such levels in our society in the past 100 years. Multiple contributing factors have brought about these shifts for entrepreneurship. In just the past 50 years, consider these trends:

• One in 5 college graduates used to work for a well-known Fortune 500 company; today it's only 1 in 11.

• To replace 35 percent of the Fortune 500 companies it used to take 20 to 25 years; today it takes 3 to 4 years.

• Half a century ago, some 200,000 companies would be started each year; now six times that number will be launched—with 1,200,000 companies starting annually.

• This movement even cuts across gender barriers. The "good 'ol boys networks" are quickly becoming a thing of the past. In the 1990s, women started and owned enterprises employing 12 million people—more than all the Fortune 500 companies combined![4]

The entrepreneurial revolution is not so silent anymore. The ripple effect of this exciting movement reaches across cultural, age, and gender gaps, spilling over into a wide diversity of enterprises—including the work of building Christ's kingdom. This new movement births new expectations and hope for a better life for many throughout our society. One entrepreneur, describing this cultural shift, invited others to join in the adventurous journey. Although he wasn't giving an altar invitation in a missionary service, he certainly echoed the pioneering spirit of the apostle Paul, didn't he?

Being an entrepreneur is for anyone who wants to experience the
deep dark canyons of uncertainty and ambiguity, and
who wants to walk the breathtaking highlands of success.
But I must caution you—
do not plan to walk the latter
until you have experienced the former.

Consider for a moment the abilities and attitudes an entrepreneurial leader can bring to the table in pioneering NewStart churches by blending a balance of missional calling with the skill sets of entrepreneurs.

QUALITIES OF EFFECTIVE ENTREPRENEURS

Jeff Timmons in his best-selling book titled *New Venture Creation* captured the key habits, practices, and attitudes of leaders in the business world who had started new companies. As a professor at Babson College and Harvard Business School, his work is renowned for training successful entrepreneurs in business. Among various common traits, Timmons emphasizes 10 shared characteristics of effective entrepreneurs. Though Timmons was not thinking about the ministry parallels, what he has to say certainly applies to missional entrepreneurs.

• **Achievement Oriented.** These leaders are hard-driving doers who are committed to excellence and achieving what they set out to do. They possess a resiliency that keeps them focused and on track regardless of the disappointments they face. What a vivid description of the attitude needed for a NewStart pastor!

• **People of Vision**. These innovators possess a strong confidence in the correctness of their vision and calling. At times they almost seemed consumed with the pursuit of their particular opportunity. As one visionary pastor says, "First you have a dream, and then with the passing of time, the dream has you!"

• **Solution Oriented**. These leaders deal with problems and setbacks in a positive manner, persisting in a situation until they get it right. Their determination fuels incredible endurance in the face of great adversities. Who can forget the perseverance of those first missional pioneers through imprisonment, beatings, trials, threats, stonings, and on and on! They must have cut "quit" out of their dictionaries!

• **Encouraging Leaders**. These revolutionaries reflect an ability to positively inspire others around them. They lift the people around them. They make heroes of others. They enlist, equip, and empower others to join them in their journey of faith in starting a new church. Mentoring is almost second nature to them, giving away ministry to trained partners.

• **A Unique Individuality**. Most of these effective leaders possessed good judgment and a sense of how the real world operates. They know themselves, they know their strengths, and they remained honest about their limitations. They're experienced in their work and have a "street smarts" perspective in working with people.

• **Lifelong Learning**. These high achievers value their life experiences as adding meaning to their personal and professional lives. For them the joy is in the journey, not just the destination. They play for the long haul, and most see any gains only as a way of gauging progress.

• **Avoid Giant Risks.** Contrary to the popular misconception, most effective entrepreneurs are uncomfortable with putting everything on the line in a new venture. They much prefer to hedge the risks and plan out a proper course of action, avoiding unnecessary hazards and accepting only the calculated risks that provide the right opportunities.

• **Keen Sense of Humor**. The high achievers are able to laugh at themselves and see the humor in their problem situations. Humor becomes a great shock absorber in their lives, creating personal resiliency for their inevitable problems. Most possess great commitment and dogged determination in crises because of their ability to balance their loads with laughter.

• **Share the Credit.** These leaders maintain a generally positive and inspirational attitude. They facilitate and encourage teamwork in their business ventures, empowering and enlisting other capable leaders along the way. This special brand of leaders shares the fruits of endeavors with those who helped produce them. Lone Rangers just don't exist in this group of movers and shakers. All of Paul's letters illustrate his groups of coworkers, friends, and partners in ministry. The New Testament is filled with references to the various networks of people, both in Christ's ministry and in the Early Church. Leaders link people clusters.

• **Self-Starting Doers**. They take up multiple tasks at the same time and can tolerate the unpredictable nature of their work. Ambiguity and unclear outcomes are acceptable risks to be taken. Complacency and contentment are strangers to their mind-set and attitudes. Many times they make incredible sacrifices in the face of unbelievable problems to reach their goals. Quite a relevant portrait of faith, wouldn't you say?

With the current practice of investigating corporate management principles, retaining New Testament models for the church and ministry remains an important focus. We dare not lose the commitment to be Kingdom pioneers who model servant leadership or pastors who shepherd their congregations with integrity and Christlikeness. To move past these biblical models of ministry in the New Testament Church pushes us beyond acceptable boundaries. Most of us don't want to go there.

At the same time, we realize large and small churches must operate from different organizational and managerial structures. We even see how the entrepreneurial spirit shows up in a number of places in the Scriptures. The same principles modeled by many business leaders today are not only complementary to scriptural truths but also described in the biblical record. The parallels almost jump off the pages of Scripture.

Jesus taught us to be "wise as serpents and harmless as doves" (Matt. 10:16, KJV). While we minister in this world, we need to be aware of our surrounding culture while remaining authentic in our faith.

James wrote that genuine faith involves more than just dreaming —it's doing something. Without action, faith is dead.

The early communities of faith that made a difference in their world constantly affirmed and uplifted each other, like a team of encouraging cheerleaders. The apostle Paul expressed it best when he wrote, "I aspired to preach the gospel, not where Christ was already named, that I might not build upon another man's foundation; but as it is written, 'They who had no news of Him shall see, and they who have not heard shall understand'" (Rom. 15:20-21, NASB).

Sounds like a Timmons description, doesn't it? Using entrepreneurial principles in the context of contemporary ministry need not be linked to negative images. Some of the principles are as old as the apostle Paul's writings and as proven as the practices of the New Testament Church.

SOME COMMON MISUNDERSTANDINGS

Timmons and other business leaders discuss several widely accepted misconceptions concerning entrepreneurs. The crossovers between Kingdom endeavors and secular business seem fairly obvious.

• **"Entrepreneurs operate in the short term."** Some critics see entrepreneurs as promoters and quick-profit artists, as they are portrayed many times in the media. Instead, the authentic entrepreneurial spirit cares equally about their tasks as well as relationships. Effective entrepreneurs and missional pioneers are a balanced blend of doers and relaters, with a keen sense of justice for doing the right thing. People and tasks carry equal importance.

• **"Entrepreneurs are too control oriented."** Too many times their desire to guide their own destiny is interpreted by some as being overly controlling. The best entrepreneurs enlist the experience and talent of those around them. Their team shares not only the responsibility but also the authority for carrying out their ministry objectives.

• **"Entrepreneurs have to be inventors."** To some, the entrepreneur must be a know-it-all generalist who creates and develops everything from scratch. The truth is, most entrepreneurs start the smaller companies that implement 95 percent of the new inventions used today—from PCs and disposable razors to frozen foods and soft contact lenses. Major Fortune 500 companies are not the ones introducing the majority of innovative products flooding today's marketplace. They usually flow from smaller, relatively unknown entrepreneurial companies.

• **"Entrepreneurs are super human."** Not only are they normal people with their own blend of strengths and weaknesses, but also 20 percent of these entrepreneurs are over the age of 40 according to recent studies. These high-impact new companies are being run not just by the young, idealistic, and highly energetic but by a wide range of diverse and capable leaders. Today, young and old, men and women, from a wide range of cultural and racial backgrounds are starting some of the strongest new churches.

These common misunderstandings make training a high priority for missional pioneers. Entrepreneurial leaders must be continual learners.

How Are Leaders Trained?

The Church of the Nazarene has a unique training strategy called the College of New Church Knowledge (CONK). CONK is a series of annual training events sponsored across the United States that focuses on multiple training tracks for pastors and lay leaders working in or planning to begin NewStart churches. CONK provides opportunities for NewStart leaders to network and exchange ideas. Most consultants agree that these skill sets can be learned. Presenters in each CONK are effective church starters who work in local NewStart ministries and share insights in the practical aspects of starting and growing strong new churches, with a special emphasis in developing entrepreneurial skills. This unique component in this NewStart strategy focuses on teaching and training in the skill sets needed for effective missional entrepreneurs.

All the various aspects of starting a new church are topics for presentations and group discussions. Multiple ministry options allow for adapting materials and training for the wide range of communities being reached. The church's benchmarks in the early years are an outstanding benefit from these days of training and interaction with other NewStart pastors. Effectively communicating the gospel message in the context of our holiness heritage engages lively discussions. Advertising methods for a new church and funding the ministry and discipleship efforts are among some of the many other topics covered. Every session includes a question-and-answer session, as well as time scheduled for panel discussions as a group. Plans are under way to make these training sessions available on-line.

What About Funding?

Obviously, money is needed to operate a church. A new church usually has a small group of people whose contributions are inadequate to provide the same financial base of an older, established church. Even if the NewStart pastor can be bivocational, other ministry overhead expenses usually carry a significant price tag. Some newer congregations are held back in their development because of inadequate financial planning. For some, sponsoring congregations provide a monthly subsidy or help with a down payment on the purchase of a more permanent meeting facility. In 100 different new-church situations, 100 different financial plans may be used to adequately assist the new church. Here are just a few financial considerations:

1. Avoid creating a long-term dependency on outside financial support. While some initial subsidy may be needed for new churches,

the sooner the subsidy ends, the better. Most subsidies reduce over a two- to three-year period. Such guidelines should be spelled out clearly for everyone—on paper. Review them annually.

2. Encourage the church to be proactive in facing their financial challenges. While the funding follows behind the attendance of new believers, a gradual increase of responsibilities of the membership builds stability and strength for the church's future. Stewardship grows with proper discipleship.

3. The more members and volunteers are helped by the church, the more they will own responsibility for the ministry. Regular updates on the progress of the church, information on the upcoming events and future goals, and the flow of information back to those financially supporting the ministry at any level will generate even greater investments in the ministry. A monthly pastoral letter to all the financial partners in the ministry goes a long way to cultivate support. Remember: return appreciation, communication, and information for greater participation.

4. "Speed of the leader equals the speed of the team." The pastoral staff and lay leadership provide examples to the rest of the congregation in stewardship values and practices. Stewardship needs to be caught as much as it is taught. People have a way of following those who set the right examples in giving.

HOW ARE LEADERS SELECTED?

The well-known axiom says, "Everything rises and falls on leadership." Pastoral choices determine effectiveness on many levels. New congregations tend to flourish or flounder depending on their initial selection of pastoral leadership. The singular, most important decision in regard to starting a new church is choosing the founding pastor. This fact guides the whole process for effectively selecting appropriate new-church leadership in the NewStart Assessment Centers. These assessments determine the suitability of a particular individual as the missional entrepreneur for a new church. Potential NewStart pastoral couples are interviewed and observed in these weeklong assessments before receiving any assignment to start a new Nazarene church. Assessment registration and materials are available by calling the NewStart toll-free number at 1-800-306-8294.

SOME INITIAL STEPS TO GETTING STARTED

So how can we activate the soul of a pastor with the savvy of an entrepreneur? Trying to summarize what we have read so far, here's how a missional NewStart pastor might incorporate these entrepreneurial principles as beginning steps in the process:

Follow God's Calling. Missional leaders are devoted to following Christ and building His kingdom. Their love for Christ and desire to obey Him serve as primary motivations in their lives. Where is it that God may be leading to start a new church? Can this new work be described to others in a convincing and attractive way so that they may want to join in the effort? Enrollment in the next Assessment Center may affirm and accelerate this miracle in the making.

Evaluate This Opportunity. Like their entrepreneurial counterpart, missional leaders must be able to accurately evaluate the specific potentials for new churches. They find out if the area really needs a new church. Are there unique problems facing a new church in this area? Missional pioneers learn to operate with their knees bent—both for prayer and flexibility!

Organize a Plan. If ambiguity characterizes earthly entrepreneurial endeavors, faith provides the spiritual ability to see what does not yet exist. From these many details in starting new churches, and dozens of others as well, the process can be started. With some prayer and proper planning, many of the high-risk areas can be reduced to more tolerable levels. Enroll in the College of New Church Knowledge. Begin developing your own network of NewStart leaders for mentoring and feedback.

Find the Resources. Although few NewStart pastors have everything they want or need for starting a new church, some kind of inventory needs to be taken of available resources. What properties may be available for starting this new church? What missing resources have to be acquired? How will they be obtained for this new church? The equipped and prepared new church is more likely to achieve lasting success.

Stay the Course. The Scriptures describe David at one point in his life where he "encouraged himself in the LORD" (1 Sam. 30:6, KJV). In the grand scheme of things, NewStart pastors learn to view life's setbacks as divine setups for God to do something new and unexpected. What strategies are in place for handling discouragement? Missional entrepreneurs learn to recharge their own spiritual batteries. How can you find ways to overcome disappointments and setbacks that would stop most leaders?

MISSIONAL ENTREPRENEURS NEEDED—NOW!

Massive populations across the United States and Canada are essentially unreached by the gospel. These unreached people make necessary the multiplication of new churches into every subculture. Addition is relatively uncomplicated. It only requires one conversion per church occasionally. But massive multiplication from new churches is needed. While certainly more challenging, adding new churches in a shorter period of time assures the greater multiplication of new believers.

As Bill Sullivan has written, "Multiplication is necessary because the size and urgency of our missional call demands it. The urgent spiritual need and the insistent commission of our Lord compels us as the Church of the Nazarene to multiply new churches across our continent among every group of people."

The challenge remains the same as our Lord described it in Matt. 9:37-38: "The harvest is plentiful, but the laborers are few; therefore ask the Lord of the harvest to send out laborers into his harvest." As an army of missional pioneers scatters across our continent launching hundreds of NewStart churches, who can predict all of the eternal consequences?

Maybe you can be one of these missional entrepreneurs. Perhaps as you have read these pages, your heart and mind have been challenged with the great potential of starting a new church. Pursue any leadings you may sense. You could play a vital role in a great movement of God across the United States and Canada through the NewStart strategy.

A casual review of denominational records indicates in the early days of the Church of the Nazarene, we started nearly one church per day! As the NewStart strategy captures our hearts and imaginations, the far-reaching ripple effect of these efforts is staggering! In the words of our founding denominational leader: "Any man who has a deep, conscientious conviction that God has called him to a work is a force to be reckoned with. When a few thousand people share that conviction and everyone shares it and strengthens it in the hearts of the other— there is no telling to what the thing may grow."[5]

Notes

Chapter 1

1. Harold Ivan Smith, comp., *The Quotable Bresee* (Kansas City: Beacon Hill Press of Kansas City, 1983), 151.
2. Neil B. Wiseman and L. Wayne Sears, comp. and ed., *Uncommon Stories from Everyday Nazarenes*, in Architects of the Enduring (Kansas City: Beacon Hill Press of Kansas City, 2001), 16.
3. Daniel Sanchez, "Strategies for Starting Churches," in *Missiology: An Introduction to the Foundations, History, and Strategies of World Missions*, ed. John Mark Terry, Ebbie Smith, and Justice Anderson (Nashville: Broadman and Holman Publishers, 1998), 473-74.
4. David J. Hesselgrave, *Planting Churches Cross-Culturally*, 2nd ed. (Grand Rapids: Baker Book House, 2000), 32.
5. *Missional Alert*, July 11, 2001.
6. *Missional Alert*, July 3, 2001.

Chapter 2

1. Chuck Van Engen, "Is the Church for Everyone?" *Journal of the American Society for Church Growth* (spring 2000): 36.
2. Manuscript available from the Mission Strategy office.

Chapter 5

1. Hesselgrave, *Planting Churches Cross-Culturally*, 51.
2. Ibid., 56.
3. Smith, *Quotable Bresee*, 99.

Chapter 6

1. David A. Aaker and Erick Joachimsthaler, marketing authors and researchers, University of California, Berkeley, in *The Quotable Executive* (New York: McGraw-Hill, 2000), 26.
2. Karen Dean Fry, "The Boilermaker Who Planted Churches: Frank Dean," in *Uncommon Stories*, 29.
3. *Core Values: Church of the Nazarene* (Kansas City: Beacon Hill Press of Kansas City, 2001), 1.
4. Ibid., 2.
5. *Core Values DVD*.
6. *Core Values*, 2.
7. *Missional Alert*, August 22, 2001.
8. *Core Values*, 2.
9. *Nazarene Messenger*, sermon, vol. 11, October 11, 1906, 3.
10. *Missional Alert*, April 25, 2001.
11. Ron Benefiel, "'Missional' Is in Our Bones," in *And Now . . . Next Door and Down the Freeway* (Kansas City: Beacon Hill Press of Kansas City, 2001), 33.
12. *Missional Alert*, August 15, 2001.

13. Tom Nees, "The Changing Face of the Church," in *And Now . . . Next Door,* 66.

14. Benefiel, *And Now . . . Next Door,* 29.

15. Bill M. Sullivan, paper, "Strategy for Developing Strong New Churches—the Right Way!" 2.

Chapter 7

1. Richard Houseal, "Women Clergy in the Church of the Nazarene: An Analysis of Change from 1908 to 1995" (master's thesis in sociology, University of Missouri-Kansas City, 1996), 22.

2. Rebecca Laird, *Ordained Women in the Church of the Nazarene: The First Generation* (Kansas City: Nazarene Publishing House, 1993), 11.

3. R. Pierce Beaver, *All Loves Excelling: American Protestant Women in World Mission* (Grand Rapids: William B. Eerdmans Publishing Company, 1968), 109.

4. Paul Cho, *More than Numbers* (Waco, Tex.: Word, 1984), 43.

5. Ibid., 44.

6. Laird, *Ordained Women,* 62-63.

7. Ibid., 63.

8. Ibid., 64.

9. "Sister Moore Starts a Holiness Church at 53," *GROW* 1, No. 1 (spring 1990): 10.

10. "Marietta First Church Sponsors West Cobb NewStart," *GROW* 10, No. 2 (summer 1999): 3.

11. Jim Dorsey, "Starter Kit for Starting Strong New Churches" (Kansas City: NewStart, Evangelism and Church Growth Division, Church of the Nazarene, 1997), 20.

12. Larry Crabb, *Men and Women* (Grand Rapids: Zondervan Publishing House, 1991), 160-61.

13. James C. Dobson, *Straight Talk* (Dallas: Word Publishing, 1991), 182.

14. Edward C. Lehman Jr., *Gender and Work: The Case of the Clergy* (Albany, N.Y.: State University of New York Press, 1993), 182.

15. Ibid., 20.

16. Ibid.

17. David Fisher, *The 21st Century Pastor* (Grand Rapids: Zondervan Publishing House, 1996), 162.

18. Smith, Ibid., 169.

19. *Quotable Bresee,* 150.

20. Laird, *Ordained Women,* 141.

21. Ibid., 140.

22. John Woods, *The Quotable Executive* (New York: McGraw-Hill, 2000), 202.

Chapter 8

1. Michael Barone, *The New Americans* (Washington, D.C.: Regnery Publishing Company, 2001), 8-12.

2. Cheryl J. Sanders, document, "Bridging the Divide: The Changing Face of the Church in the Light of the Scriptures," 1998.

3. Tom Nees, document, "Building an Inclusive Church in a Multicultural Society" (Manuscript available from the Mission Strategy Office).

4. Mark Chaves, *National Congregations Study*, machine-readable file, Department of Sociology, University of Arizona, 1999.

5. Hesselgrave, *Planting Churches Cross-Culturally*, 35.

6. Carl S. Dudley, *Basic Steps Toward Community Ministry* (Alban Institute, 1991).

7. Manuel Ortiz, *One New People: Models for Developing a Multiethnic Church* (Downers Grove, Ill.: InterVarsity Press, 1996), 125.

8. William Smalley, "The World Is Too Much with Us: Readings in Missionary Anthropology II," *Practical Anthropology* (1967), 702.

9. Robert M. Franklin, *Another Day's Journey* (Minneapolis: Fortress Press, 1997), 122-24.

Chapter 9

1. Fry, "Boilermaker," 29.

2. *The Communicator's Commentary, Acts* (Waco, Tex.: Word, 1983), 57.

3. Harnack, *The Reconstruction of the Church—on What Pattern?* (Nashville: Abingdon, 1970), 43-46.

4. Charles Van Engen, *God's Missionary People: Rethinking the Purpose of the Local Church* (Grand Rapids: Baker Book House, 1991), 153.

5. Ibid., 176.

6. V. H. Lewis, *The Church Winning Souls* (Kansas City: Beacon Hill Press of Kansas City, 1983), 67.

7. Howard A. Snyder, *The Radical Wesley and Patterns for Church Renewal* (Downers Grove, Ill.: InterVarsity Press, 1980), 63.

Chapter 10

1. Gene Wilkes, *Jesus on Leadership* (Wheaton, Ill.: Tyndale House Publishers, 1998), 127.

2. C. Peter Wagner, *Church Planting for a Greater Harvest* (Ventura, Calif.: Regal, 1990), 8-12.

3. Jeff Timmons, *The Keys to Entrepreneurial Success*, Harvard Business Video Series, Scott/Tyler Productions, 1996, videocassette.

4. Ibid.

5. Smith, *The Quotable Bresee*, 86.